MARXISM IN POWER

THE RISE AND FALL OF A DOCTRINE

MICHAEL G. KORT

THE MILLBROOK PRESS
BROOKFIELD, CONNECTICUT

Published by The Millbrook Press
2 Old New Milford Road
Brookfield, Connecticut 06804

Library of Congress Cataloging-in-Publication Data

Kort, Michael G., 1944–
Marxism in power : the rise and fall of a doctrine / Michael Kort.
p.   cm.
Includes bibliographical references and index.
Summary: Traces the development of Marxism, its rise to power in
the Soviet Union and elsewhere, and the factors that led to the
collapse of Marxist governments in the late 1980s and early 1990s.
ISBN 1-56294-241-7 (lib. bdg.)
1. Communism—History—Juvenile literature.   2. Marx, Karl,
1818–1883—Influence—History—Juvenile literature.   3. Utopian
socialism—History—Juvenile literature.   [1. Communism—History.
2. Marx, Karl, 1818–1883—Influence—History.]   I. Title.
HX36.K657   1993
335.43—dc20   92-15697   CIP   AC

CONTENTS

Chapter One
Workers of the World, What Happened? 7

Chapter Two
Socialism Before Marx 12

Chapter Three
Karl Marx and Marxism 22

Chapter Four
Lenin and Bolshevism 45

Chapter Five
Marxism and Stalinism 74

Chapter Six
Soviet Marxism After Stalin 94

Chapter Seven
Chinese Marxism and Maoism   106

Chapter Eight
The Fringes of Marxism   132

Chapter Nine
Crisis and Collapse   147

Notes   166

Suggested Reading   169

Chronology   171

Index   173

For Florence and Jack,
the radical ones

Karl Marx.

CHAPTER ONE

WORKERS OF THE WORLD, WHAT HAPPENED?

On November 7, 1989, the Union of Soviet Socialist Republics celebrated the anniversary of the Bolshevik Revolution. As it did each year on that day, the Soviet government sponsored large parades and elaborate ceremonies across the length and breadth of the world's largest country. The events commemorated the day in 1917 when the Bolshevik Party had seized power in the country then known as Russia, with the goal of building the first society in the world based on the ideas of Karl Marx.

A nineteenth-century German philosopher, Marx had been a fierce critic of capitalism, the dominant economic system in Europe and the rest of the Western world. He was a passionate advocate of socialism or communism, two terms which in the mid-nineteenth century often were used interchangeably to describe a type of ideal society. Marx believed that capitalism, based on private ownership of property and the free-market system, allowed a lucky few to become very rich while condemning the overwhelming majority to grinding poverty. According to Marx, a socialist system, based on public ownership of all wealth and a planned economic system, would ensure a good life for all.

In 1848, in a pamphlet known as *The Communist Manifesto*, Marx and his close friend and collaborator Friedrich Engels boldly predicted the collapse of capitalism throughout Europe and its replacement by socialism. They ended their book with their famous rallying cry, "Workers of all countries, unite." Marx and Engels hoped that the factory workers of Europe would get together and seize control of a large part of the continent, end capitalism and its injustices, and build a socialist society. Neither Marx, who died in 1883, nor Engels, who died in 1895, lived to see capitalism overthrown anywhere. But after the dawn of a new century, in 1917, a group of Marxists gained control of Russia and began to try to put the ideals of *The Communist Manifesto* into practice.

For much of the twentieth century, Marxism seemed to be the wave of the future. The Marxists who seized control in Russia at the end of World War I renamed the country the Union of Soviet Socialist Republics and, during the next two decades, transformed it from a largely agricultural society into an industrial giant. Confidence in Soviet socialism and Marxism grew both at home and abroad. Many intellectuals in Western Europe and the United States were attracted to Marxism. In the 1930s, with the capitalist countries of the West locked in the grip of the Great Depression, a group of intellectuals from England visited the USSR, proclaiming afterward that they "had seen the future and it works." World War II, which lasted from 1939 to 1945, led to more Marxist victories. Marxist regimes, largely with the help of the Soviet army, came to power in Eastern Europe after 1945. In 1949, Marxists won a bloody civil war in China. With the victory in China, both the country with the largest territory in the world— the USSR—and the country with the most people in the world—China—were ruled by followers of Karl Marx.

Countries in Africa, Asia, and the Americas were taken over by Marxists during the 1950s, 1960s, and 1970s, including Angola, Vietnam, Cuba, and Nicaragua. By then well over a third of the human race lived under Marxist regimes, and those countries produced about 40 percent of the world's industrial goods. During the 1950s and 1960s the economy of the USSR, the world's first and leading Marxist nation, grew at a faster rate than that of the United States, the world's greatest capitalist power. And in 1957, the USSR stunned the United States and the world by launching the world's first artificial satellite. When Nikita Khrushchev, the leader of the USSR from 1953 to 1964, remarked to a group of Americans, "We will bury you," many people in both the USSR and the United States believed he was right. Even in many countries where Marxists were not in power, such as Italy, France, and India, they formed powerful political parties that could not be ignored.

Yet 72 years after the Bolshevik Revolution and 141 years after the publication of The Communist Manifesto, five thousand Soviet citizens held their

**Moscow demonstrators burn a copy of *Pravda*,
the Communist Party newspaper, in 1989.**

own rally on November 7, the day Soviet citizens normally celebrated the victory of Marxism and socialism in their country. They marched through the streets of Moscow, the country's capital, with protest signs, including one that read, "Workers of the world, we're sorry." Marxism, they insisted, was a complete failure. Despite an enormous effort by millions of people that had required great suffering and deprivation, three quarters of a century of Marxist socialism had left the USSR poor, hungry, and generally miserable.

In fact, by the late 1980s, Marxism was in retreat almost everywhere. The five thousand people who demonstrated in Moscow against Marxism on November 7, 1989, obviously were a tiny minority of the people in the USSR. Yet their view that Marxism had failed represented the majority opinion in a country where for seven decades it literally had been a crime to disagree with the basic ideas of Marxism. And while these protesters challenged Marxism in Moscow, Marxist governments were under challenge or were collapsing around the world. Barely two years later, in 1991, Marxism collapsed in the Soviet Union, whereupon the Soviet Union itself disintegrated.

What had happened? Why was Marxism so appealing to so many people for so long? How were Marxists able to come to power in large and important countries like Russia and China? What did they accomplish, and fail to accomplish, once they were in control? What went wrong, and why was the decline of Marxism so swift and so total? These and other questions about one of the most important doctrines of our time form the subject of this book.

CHAPTER TWO

SOCIALISM BEFORE MARX

Socialism is a modern word that did not come into use until the 1820s. Since then the term has been used by many people, including Karl Marx, to describe varying visions of how to organize society. However, most people would agree that the word socialism does mean at least a few key things.

Socialists reject the capitalist system, in particular the idea that an economic system should be based on competition between individuals. They believe that cooperation is a more humane and efficient way to produce and distribute the goods that people need to live. Socialists also oppose the unplanned nature of capitalism, where individuals working for themselves and their personal profit decide what to produce. They maintain that it is more efficient and productive to plan for the entire society, based on what is good for it as a whole.

Socialists also believe in equality. This generally means that every member of a society should have approximately the same share of the material goods a society produces. It does not necessarily mean that everyone should participate in deciding how things should be run. Some socialists believed in democracy, while others were convinced that only the most intelligent and best educated people should make the important decisions that governed a society. The non-democratic socialists argued that as long as food, housing, and other material goods were distributed equally, it did not matter if a society was run in a dictatorial way.

Apart from a fair distribution of goods, equality would have another important benefit: it would eliminate the social divisions and strife that have plagued all other types of societies, from the slave-holding societies of the ancient world to the modern European capitalist states.

PRE-SOCIALIST THINKERS AND ACTIVISTS

Socialist theorists such as Karl Marx drew many of their ideas from earlier philosophers, some of whom wrote as far back as ancient times. Perhaps the most important of these ancient Western thinkers was the Greek philosopher Plato. In the fourth century B.C. he described his ideal society in The Republic.

Plato's goal was to establish an orderly society that would be free of the turmoil that had ravaged his beloved Athens and led it to disaster against the rival city-state of Sparta in the Peloponnesian War (431–404 B.C.). He began by rejecting Athenian de-

mocracy. Plato's republic would be ruled by spe-
cially trained "philosopher-kings" whose decisions
everyone would have to obey. Plato believed that all
individual interests had to be subordinated to the
greater communal good, and his concept of placing
community above individual needs was at the core
of much socialist thinking more than two thousand
years later.

Another influential pre-socialist thinker was the
Englishman Sir Thomas More (1478–1535). More
gave a new word to the English language when he
imagined an ideal society on an island he called
Utopia. While today the word *utopia* implies a society or organization so perfect that it can never exist, More's detailed description of how his island
community worked was so convincing that many
people of his time actually believed it existed and
tried to find it. They might have spared themselves
a lot of trouble had they looked up the Greek meaning of the word *utopia*, which is "no place."

The key to Utopia's success was that all wealth
was shared. This would eliminate poverty and crime.
Unlike citizens of Plato's republic, those of More's
Utopia enjoyed freedom of thought and elected their
rulers. Another important feature was the work day,
which was only six hours long, as opposed to work
days in Europe that often lasted fourteen hours in
More's time. In addition, farming, which More considered to be the most difficult and least pleasant
work of all, was divided among all Utopia's citizens. More's own fate was distinctly un-utopian.
Caught in the fury of the Protestant Reformation in
England, he defied King Henry VIII and remained
loyal to the Catholic Church. As a result, he was
convicted of treason and beheaded.

Two hundred years later, across the English Channel in France, Jean-Jacques Rousseau continued the search for a perfect society. Rousseau argued that man was naturally good; it was the unfair way society was organized that made people commit crimes and otherwise behave badly. He summed up his views in the famous sentence, "Man was born free, and everywhere he is in chains." Rousseau attacked many aspects of the French society of his day, but his most bitter criticism was reserved for private property. It, above all, Rousseau believed, led to the unfair distribution of wealth and many of the disastrous circumstances that he wanted to correct. Rousseau's solution, like Plato's, was to put community interests above individual concerns. Rousseau recommended that everyone be subordinated to what he called the "General Will." Exactly how the General Will would be determined or how it would work in practice he did not make clear. All that was clear was that it would *not* be through parliaments and democracy, neither of which Rousseau trusted.

While Plato, More, and Rousseau contributed primarily *ideas* to the socialist heritage, a fiery Frenchman named François Noël Babeuf (1760–1797) contributed a heroic example of fighting and dying for the cause. Babeuf was actively involved in the French Revolution. When, after 1794, the leadership of the revolution became more conservative and tried to restore order, Babeuf organized a conspiracy to seize power called the "conspiracy of equals." The group's most important document, *Manifesto of Equals*, stated simply and directly: "Men are equal. This is a self-evident truth. As soon say that it is night when the sun shines, as deny this."[1]

Babeuf called on the poor people of France to seize control of the country, abolish private property, and create a society where everyone was absolutely equal. After the conspiracy was discovered, he was executed. But his ideas continued to live among his followers and later idealists.

UTOPIAN SOCIALISTS

The term *utopian socialists* refers primarily to three thinkers whose careers spanned the late eighteenth and early nineteenth centuries: Frenchmen Claude Henri Saint-Simon and Charles Fourier and Englishman Robert Owen. None of them called themselves "utopian"; that was a label Marx and Engels stuck on them later to imply that they were unrealistic and muddleheaded. All three occupy a major place in the history of socialist thought.

Saint-Simon, Fourier, and Owen developed their ideas in response to a changing world. During the late eighteenth and early nineteenth centuries much of Europe was swept by two great overlapping revolutions: the French Revolution and the Industrial Revolution. The French Revolution had an enduring influence in Europe. It overthrew Western Europe's most powerful monarchy and swept away privileges that the French nobility and clergy had enjoyed for hundreds of years. Its message of liberty and equality, and the idea that ordinary people could get together and take their fate into their own hands, thundered across the continent.

The Industrial Revolution began earlier and proceeded at a slower pace, but was even more unstoppable than the French Revolution. It started after

1750 in England and by 1830 transformed that island nation into the world's first industrial society. The rest of Western Europe and the United States lagged behind, but by the mid-nineteenth century the changes brought about by modern industry were in evidence throughout the Western world.

The Industrial Revolution created the potential for a better material life for everyone in Europe. For example, Britain produced seventeen times more cotton cloth in 1830 than in 1796. This meant that there was much more cloth to go around, and at a higher quality and lower price than before. And what was true for cotton was true for other goods.

The problem was that all this production came at a terrible human cost. The work day in the new factories was as long as sixteen hours. Because women and children were easy to control and would work for low wages, they often were the preferred labor force. Frequently the children were as young as five or six years old when they entered the factories. They were subjected not only to long hours in dimly lit and poorly heated workshops, but frequently to severe beatings.

Morever, as tens of thousands of people seeking work crowded into mushrooming towns, basic needs such as housing and sanitation went unmet. Squalid slums blighted England's cities and towns. Family life disintegrated as craftsmen were unable to compete with the new factories that employed their wives and children at miserably low wages.

Against this grim background, some people concluded that capitalism had to be replaced. Saint-Simon (1760–1825) was a French count who had fought with the colonists against the British during the American Revolution. He did not participate in the French Revolution, but he felt that he had important contributions to make to the world. He claimed to be a descendant of the great medieval emperor Charlemagne and ordered his servant to waken him each morning by saying, "Remember, Monsieur le Comte, you have great things to do."

Saint-Simon's vision of the ideal society had two main socialist qualities: its economy would be carefully planned, and all industrial equipment and important economic assets would be publicly owned. Recognizing the importance of the Industrial Revolution, he argued that society should be controlled by engineers and other technically skilled individuals who understood modern technology and industry. As he put it unapologetically:

> The industrial class should occupy the first rank, because it is the most important of all; because it can do without the others, while none of the others can do without it; because it exists by its own force, by its personal labors. The other classes ought to work for it because they are its creatures and because it maintains their existence.[2]

Saint-Simon did not confine his vision to France. He was a man whose giant schemes reached to distant lands; he proposed, for example, to dig a canal at the narrow isthmus called Suez in Egypt where Asia met Africa.

Saint-Simon never got to carry out any of his schemes, and his personal fortunes declined during his later years. Unable to earn a living or get his books published, he had to turn to his family for support. He began to despair and even attempted suicide. But his ideas grew in influence across Europe after he died.

Charles Fourier (1772–1837) agreed with Rousseau that man was basically good and that in a properly organized society happiness could be universal. His vision of a perfect society was based on communal units, each made up of about 1,600 people, housed in buildings called phalansteries. Fourier provided precise designs for the phalansteries and descriptions of how the various groups in these communities would interrelate. Because his communities would be so efficient and fair, everyone would have to work only a few hours per day. He even had a solution for the problem of who would do the grimy and dirty work most people shunned: It would be done by children, who naturally enjoyed getting as filthy as they could.

At some point Fourier's mental stability began to suffer. His predictions included the calculations that the world would last exactly 80,000 years, individuals would live 144 years, and the moon would be replaced by six new satellites. He also believed that the sea would someday turn to lemonade. Fourier, who was unsuccessful in business, was certain that there were wealthy patrons willing to finance his schemes. For ten years he made himself available every day at noon for such a person. But nobody came.

Despite these flights of fancy, Fourier's ideas attracted followers, including some in the United States. A number of socialist communities were based on his ideas, the most famous of which was Brook

THE CRISIS,

OR THE CHANGE FROM ERROR AND MISERY, TO TRUTH AND HAPPINESS

1832.

IF WE CANNOT YET

LET US ENDEAVOUR

RECONCILE ALL OPINIONS,

TO UNITE ALL HEARTS.

IT IS OF ALL TRUTHS THE MOST IMPORTANT, THAT THE CHARACTER OF MAN IS FORMED FOR—NOT BY HIMSELF.

Design of a Community of 2,000 Persons, founded upon a principle, commended by Plato, Lord Bacon, Sir T. More, & R. Owen.

EDITED BY

ROBERT OWEN AND ROBERT DALE OWEN·

London:

PRINTED AND PUBLISHED BY J. EAMONSON, 15, CHICHESTER PLACE, GRAY'S INN ROAD.
STRANGE, PATERNOSTER ROW. PURKISS, OLD COMPTON STREET, AND MAY BE HAD OF ALL BOOKSELLERS.

The Crisis, a journal co-edited by Robert Owen and his son Robert Dale Owen, advocated reorganizing industry into cooperatives.

Farm in Massachusetts. Most of them failed within a few years, although one managed to survive financially for about ninety years by running a hotel.

The most practical of the utopian socialists was Robert Owen (1771–1858). He came from a working class family in Wales and, having worked since the age of nine, was able to set up his own small spinning mill in the booming English industrial town of Manchester. He was so successful that he was hired by a larger firm to manage a mill with hundreds of employees. By the age of twenty-eight he was the co-owner of the largest mill in New Lanark, Scotland, and a wealthy man.

Owen was appalled by the working conditions in Manchester, New Lanark, and all over Britain. He bought out his New Lanark partners, and then reorganized not only the factory but the entire community. Under Owen's management, working and living conditions improved drastically. The work day shrank from seventeen to ten hours. Children went to school, families lived in decent houses with more than one room, and sanitation facilities and gardens were built. Best of all, Owen still made money.

Owen's New Lanark was not a democracy. He made the decisions, about wages and working conditions as well as about penalties for drunkenness and other vices. Soon he tried to spread his ideas beyond New Lanark. Among his projects was New Harmony, Indiana—but, like the other utopian communities in the United States, New Harmony failed. Owen lost most of his fortune when it collapsed. When he died in 1858, it was as a poor man who had returned to finish his days in a small house next door to his birthplace in Wales.

CHAPTER THREE

KARL MARX AND MARXISM

While there were many socialist thinkers before Karl Marx and many more after him, none have had anything approaching his influence. His ideas about socialism became so important that they gave birth to their own term: Marxism. But Marxism was not only about socialism. It explained the evolution of human society from earliest times, including the reasons why there were rich and poor and conflict in all societies. It was also a resounding affirmation that the future was bright, that socialism not only was the best way to live but would inevitably come to pass.

MARX AND ENGELS

Karl Marx was born in 1818 in Trier, a city in the Rhineland region of western Germany. In those days

Germany was divided into many states of varying size. Trier belonged to the largest and most powerful German state, Prussia. Like most European states of the time, Prussia was an undemocractic society ruled by a powerful monarch. The people had no real influence on their government, and some of them faced special discrimination, particularly Jews. Both of Marx's grandfathers were rabbis, but when Karl was six years old his father converted the family to Christianity to escape the discrimination and legal barriers Jews faced in Prussia.

As a youth Karl was close to and influenced by two men: his father, Heinrich, and his neighbor Ludwig von Westphalen. Heinrich Marx was a well-educated and cultured man of liberal political views. Westphalen, an important government official, was very impressed with Karl's extraordinary intelligence and helped introduce him to classics of European literature. Westphalen had another asset: a daughter named Jenny, whom Karl loved from an early age and who eventually became his wife. During their life together, which lasted almost forty years until Jenny's death in 1881, they often experienced poverty and hardship, but they always loved each other deeply. Karl and Jenny Marx would have five children, three of whom died in childhood.

It would have seemed that the brilliant young Karl Marx was well suited to following his father and becoming a successful lawyer or perhaps a university professor. Karl did well in school and in 1835 enrolled in the law faculty at the University of Bonn. The following year he transferred to the University of Berlin to study philosophy. At Berlin Marx was attracted to a group of students heavily influenced by the German philosopher George Wilhelm Friedrich Hegel, who had taught at the university a few years earlier. The students liked to call themselves "the Free Ones." Although Hegel was a conservative, they used his ideas about history to develop radical ideas about freedom and became sharp critics of the Prussian regime. Marx paid a high price for his political activity: When he received his doctoral degree in 1841, he was unable to get an academic job.

Karl turned to journalism to make a living and became the editor of a newspaper called the *Rheinische Zeitung (The Rhine Newspaper)* in 1842. The job lasted five months, until the newspaper was closed down by the Prussian government because of its liberal views. With no more prospects in Prussia, Karl and his new wife Jenny abandoned their homeland in 1843 and moved to France, where they settled in Paris. There, where the memory and ideals of the French Revolution were stronger than anywhere in Europe, Marx's thinking evolved.

The most important person Marx met in Paris was a fellow German, Friedrich Engels. The lifelong friendship was a tribute to the truism that opposites attract. Marx was a sullen man who both dazzled those he met with his brilliance and repelled them with his arrogance and sarcasm. Engels, the son of a wealthy textile manufacturer, was athletic and outgoing. Whereas Marx struggled to express his incredibly complex thoughts on paper, Engels wrote easily and clearly. While Marx struggled to master spoken English, Engels was fluent in English and French and knew more than a dozen other languages. As the son of a wealthy man, Engels also

**Friedrich Engels, Marx's lifelong
friend and associate.**

knew and enjoyed the finer things in life, despite his socialist ideals. His family wealth and his position as a manager for his father provided him with a good income. On his earnings as a journalist, Marx probably would not have been able to support his wife and children had it not been for Engels's help, which began while the two men were in Paris and continued for the rest of Marx's life.

The Marx-Engels partnership probably endured because of something Engels lacked: He did not have Marx's gigantic ego. As Engels put it, "Marx was a genius. The rest of us were talented at best." Engels was being unfair to himself. The essential ideas of Marxism certainly came from Marx, but Engels contributed to their development.

When he arrived in Paris, Marx, unlike Engels, still was not a socialist. During the early 1840s in Germany, in fact, Marx had decided that the solution to most political and social problems was universal voting rights. But in Paris he arrived at a larger and grander solution to the ills of his time and of all time: socialist revolution.

Over the next several years Marx and Engels developed their fundamental ideas and wrote a number of important works. One of the best known is Engels's *Condition of the Working Class in England 1844*, a devastating exposé of working conditions in Manchester, where Engels's father owned a factory. Marx, now a convinced socialist, wrote a number of major works that outlined his evolving moral critique of capitalism. Together the two partners produced a six-hundred-page volume called *The German Ideology*. Like several of Marx's other earlier works, it was not published until the 1900s.

MARX AND THE
REVOLUTIONS OF 1848

Marx's writings and those of other German radicals
and socialists living in Paris soon led to trouble. One
of the targets of Marx's criticism was his native
Prussia. In 1845, the Prussian government convinced French authorities to expel Marx from the
country. He moved to Brussels, the capital of Bel-
gium. Soon Marx and Engels were members of a
newly formed group of German exiles called the
Communist League. In 1847, the league asked them
to compose a statement, or manifesto, about the
group's beliefs. The Communist Manifesto began with
the fierce and soon-to-be-famous warning, "A spectre
is haunting Europe—the spectre of communism." But
when it was published in early January 1848, hardly
anyone paid attention. Far more newsworthy events
were about to take place elsewhere. In February,
disturbances began in Paris that heralded the start
of the revolutions of 1848. They soon swept out-
ward from France and engulfed most of western and
central Europe.

Marx had written, "The philosophers hitherto
have only interpreted the world, in various ways;
the point, however, is to change it."[1] Now he got
his only real chance to experience rather than merely
write about revolution. After the fall of the conservative French government, he went to Paris and
then to the German city of Cologne, a hotbed of revolutionary activity. There he became editor of a new
newspaper called the Neue Rheinische Zeitung (The
New Rhine Newspaper). Marx was in Cologne during June, when the workers of Paris rose up in what

may be called Europe's first genuinely socialist uprising. Many of them were followers of Louis-Auguste Blanqui, who advocated a socialist dictatorship. Marx fervently supported the Paris workers in his newspaper, but his support was of no help as they were defeated after three days of fighting.

Soon the rising tide of repression washed over Marx as well, although with far less force. By 1849, revolutionary forces were being defeated everywhere. The Prussian government was able to restore order in Cologne, and Marx was arrested and put on trial for sedition. He did not flinch from his commitment to the revolution but made a long and brilliant speech about political and social conditions in Europe. To his and everyone else's surprise he was acquitted. The jury foreman who announced the verdict thanked the accused for such an instructive lecture. Unimpressed but legally unable to jail Marx, the Prussian government expelled him from the country. After a short stay in Paris, Marx arrived at the age of thirty-two in London, where he was to spend the rest of his life.

Life was difficult for the Marxes in London. They lived in poverty, usually depending on money from Engels. Beyond his personal problems, Marx suffered continual political disappointments. A German and a socialist, he was forced to live in England, the thriving center of capitalism. A man who wanted to change the world, he lived in obscurity, writing journalistic and political articles, and doing his research. The research was done at the British Museum and in 1867 resulted in the first volume of his great work *Capital*, which carefully analyzed the evolution of capitalism. (Engels would edit and publish the second and third volumes after Marx's death.) It was through *Capital* and other works written in London that Marx, with Engels's help, laid the basis for the doctrine that bears his name.

THE FUNDAMENTAL CONCEPTS OF MARXISM

The roots of Marxism lie deep in the intellectual soil of Western culture and civilization. Marx drew from the French socialist tradition, from English economists who had studied their country's industrial revolution, and from the German philosophical tradition that had produced the ideas of Hegel.

On a deeper level, he drew from the ideas of the European Enlightenment of the eighteenth century, especially the idea that understanding the world required reason and a careful examination of the facts. At the bedrock level, however, Marx drew from the Judeo-Christian commitment to social justice and compassion. Marx himself fiercely rejected religion as something that fooled human beings into concentrating on the world to come instead of doing something about life in *this* world—in the famous phrase, "Religion is the opium of the people." He was especially harsh on Judaism, the religion of his ancestors. In public and especially in private writings, he attacked Judaism in shockingly bigoted terms. But in an important sense, Marxism fundamentally is based on moral outrage at injustice and on the promise of a better world to come, much like the biblical tradition he claimed to reject.

Dialectics

Marxism begins with an assumption of the way historical change occurs. The source of Marx's view was

Hegel, who wrote that change in history occurs according to a pattern, which he called "dialectical." According to the dialectical view of history, no situation or condition—the "thesis"—can remain the same. By its very existence, it creates forces—called the "antithesis"—that are its opposite. The change occurs as the thesis and antithesis come into conflict. The old order is destroyed and gives birth to a new order—the "synthesis." But change does not stop. The new order produces the seeds of its own destruction, and the process repeats itself.

If all this sounds a bit complicated, imagine a situation in a typical family. Although parents have absolute control over their infant children, this situation (the thesis) cannot remain unchanged as the children grow older (the antithesis). This development inevitably leads to conflict, as most adolescents and their parents will attest. The conflict leads to the destruction of the old order, as growing young adults make more and more of their own decisions. Eventually a new situation arises (the synthesis): Children become independent adults, and parents and children relate on a new basis. But there is no rest, for the process immediately begins again. The newly independent adults get married, have children of their own, and—no surprise—their children eventually won't listen to them either!

Hegel's dialectic, while providing a framework for change, was unsatisfactory to Marx. To Hegel, historical change was the result of the evolution of a "World Spirit," a process which led to the development of human freedom. Making things worse, Hegel had an odd view of freedom, which he saw embodied in the repressive Prussian state. To Marx, who hated the Prussian monarchy, this made no sense at all. More importantly, to accept Hegel's view about the World Spirit meant believing that humans had no control over their destinies. This was totally unacceptable to Marx. He set out to bring Hegel's dialectic out of the spiritual world and into the physical one, and to apply it in a way that would be practical and useful to human beings.

Historical Materialism

Marx brought Hegel down to earth (Marx said that he stood Hegel "on his feet") with the concept of historical materialism. Historical materialism simply meant that history could be explained only by examining what human beings did in the real—or material—world. The *pattern* of change was, as Hegel suggested, dialectical. As with the relationship between children and their parents, every human condition produced the seeds of its own destruction. As it did so, there was conflict and struggle. Eventually the struggle produced a new condition, which in turn began to change.

Historical materialism stressed that the most important thing about any society was the way people produced what they needed—in other words, its economic base. A society could be based on hunters who used animals for food and clothing, farmers who used tools to sow and reap, or modern industry in which people produced goods with machines. Whatever techniques and technology were used, Marx called the process of getting what a society needed to survive its *mode of production* or *substructure*. Of course, the substructure of a society could be more complex; both hunting and farming, or both farming and industry, might provide what was needed. The tools and materials a society used to produce its needs, such as spears, land, plows, or machines, were the *means of production*. They also were the only significant form of *property*.

The mode of production included another essential element, which Marx called the relations of production. That term referred to who *owned* the tools or materials that produced a society's wealth. For example, in one society the actual farming might have been done by slaves or serfs, but land that produced the food belonged to the landowners. In another, the labor might have been done by workers in a factory, but the factory itself belonged to the factory owner. This situation, in which individuals rather than society as a whole owned the means of production, created what Marx called *private property*. To him, the crucial point about private property was that it led to an unequal division of the things that a society produced. For example, the landowner got most of the food produced on his land, while the factory owner owned the products produced in his factory. Private property thus divided society into what Marx called *classes,* one of which— such as the landowners in a farming society—had almost everything while the rest had almost nothing.

No society was complete without what Marx called the *superstructure.* The superstructure consisted of laws, customs, religious beliefs, political ideas, and institutions such as government. All of these protected the classes that owned the wealth and enjoyed the privileges. For example, in a society where most people were miserably poor, religion might teach that it was not this world that mattered, but the next. Thus the poor would lack the justification to demand a greater share of the wealth. Or a society might have harsh laws to punish any person who challenged the idea that a serf should work without pay for a landlord. If a society was ruled by a king, it might teach that the king ruled by divine right. Therefore, anyone who challenged the monarch's right to rule would be violating the laws of god as well as the laws of man.

Class Struggle

Despite all these barriers, change was unavoidable, however slow it might be in coming, and no ruling class was safe from it. Marx held that the superstructure of any society was originally set up to support those who did the most important work. For example, in a society where hunters fed the population, laws and customs would give them the greatest privileges. This state of affairs could last for centuries, or even longer. But change was inevitable, mainly because people were always looking for a way to make things better. And even a simple invention, over time, could change the way a society operated. Thus the invention of a primitive hoe might disrupt a society dominated by hunters by making farming a more reliable way to raise food. Gradually, more and more people would switch from hunting to farming. In other words, the substructure would change. But the old beliefs and customs—the superstructure—still would assign society's most important privileges to the hunters. This imbalance between the substructure and superstructure would intensify the conflict that Marx called *class struggle*, with the farmers slowly gaining strength at the expense of the hunters. Finally, the farmers would overthrow the hunters and establish a new superstructure of laws, customs, beliefs, and institutions that confirmed their power. And then the process of change would begin again.

It was class struggle, therefore, that brought change to society, by shifting power from one group to another. As Marx put it, "The history of all hitherto existing society is the history of class struggles."[2] This history had brought mankind through several historical phases: the primitive tribal "gens," ancient slavery, feudalism, and finally capitalism. At the gens level, there were no classes because primitive groups eked out a living by hunting and gathering, and there was nothing left over for anyone to control. With the rise of agriculture, which created a surplus for the first time, inequality and classes evolved. According to Marx, this stage was based on slave labor, with the obvious class division being between slaves and slaveowners. Next feudalism evolved, the key class division being between serfs and landlords. Gradually, within serfdom, a new class evolved, based on the growth of trade. This merchant class grew into a class called the *bourgeoisie*, which eventually overthrew the feudal lords and established a new economic system known as capitalism.

MARX'S ANALYSIS OF CAPITALISM

Although capitalism during Marx's time was an extremely harsh system, in one important sense Marx welcomed it. The great technological advances that came with the Industrial Revolution and the factory

Marx wrote that society passed through distinct phases
marked by class struggles. In the feudal phase, serfs
worked on farms owned by wealthy landowners.

system had created the ability to produce unprecedented wealth. This was essential to the eventual establishment of socialism, because only in a wealthy society with enough to go around could there be equality.

Capitalism's great flaw, as Marx saw it, was that this wealth was unevenly distributed. This was because the means of production—the machines, factories, and mines—were under the control of one small class—the bourgeoisie. Those who labored in the factories and mines and actually produced the wealth—the *proletariat*—received barely enough to stay alive. What was happening was explained by Marx's concept of *surplus value*. Surplus value was based on the *labor theory of value*, which said that the value of any product was based on the amount of labor it took to make it. (Marx considered machines and raw materials to be labor in stored form.)

For example, a table might be worth fifty dollars because fifty dollars of labor went into it. The capitalist therefore would sell it for fifty dollars. But the worker would be paid less than fifty dollars. His pay would be what he needed to stay alive, which might be twenty dollars. That would leave the capitalist with a surplus of thirty dollars (less, of course, the value of the wood and tools—the stored labor—required to build the table). This would keep the proletariat (the working class) poor, and allow the capitalists to get rich. Marx called this systematic unfairness *exploitation*.

Capitalism oppressed the proletariat in yet another way, through a process Marx called *alienation*. Marx felt that work should be satisfying, providing people with a sense of fulfillment and helping to develop their potential. Before the Industrial

Revolution, Marx said, at least some individuals did work they could take pride in, such as craftsmen who produced quality goods. But with the advent of the factory system, work was reduced to simple monotonous tasks. People worked only to get enough money to stay alive. This was alienating work, and the more of it one did, the less fulfilled one was. When alienation was added to exploitation, it produced, according to Marx, the most dehumanizing system of work in human history.

The good news in all of this, Marx said, was that it could not go on forever. To stay competitive and remain in business, capitalists would have to lower their costs. This would require using modern machines that produced goods more efficiently than human workers. But capitalists could not get surplus value—that is, profits—out of machines because they would have to pay full value for any machines they bought, just like anyone else who buys a product.

In other words, as the capitalists used more machines and fewer workers in the struggle to stay in business, their profits would inevitably fall. Then two things would happen at once: Workers would lose their jobs and see their living conditions deteriorate, and more and more capitalists would be forced out of business and down into the working class.

THE SOCIALIST REVOLUTION

Meanwhile, the working class, even as it suffered, would gain valuable experience and knowledge. The most important thing the proletariat would learn was that work in factories was a cooperative effort. To produce products, or wealth, a factory depended on everybody working together. Why, then, should the bourgeoisie get most of the wealth? In other words, the proletariat would become aware of its real interests, despite what the laws, customs, and religion of society said. This realization of what people have in common, which is taught by the experience of life itself, Marx called *class consciousness*.

As class consciousness developed, the pressure for change would build, especially as the ranks of the bourgeoisie decreased and those of the proletariat increased. Eventually the workers would be further unified when sympathetic intellectuals, whom Marx called *communists*, stepped in to lead the proletariat's struggle. The working class would then unite, overthrow the tiny capitalist minority, and abolish capitalism. This would not be achieved with violence—the bourgeoisie, like any ruling class, would not yield power voluntarily. But because the working class was so much larger, Marx had no doubt that the proletariat would triumph.

The next step would be to build a socialist society based on the cooperative work system that already existed in the factories. That job would fall to what Marx called the *dictatorship of the proletariat*. Marx had no use for democracy—he felt that elections and parliaments were tools the bourgeoisie used to mislead the workers. But the dictatorship of the proletariat would not be a traditional dictatorship because the overwhelming majority, acting together, would suppress only the former oppressors.

The dictatorship of the proletariat would reorganize society to get ready for socialism. At this point

Marx distinguished between *socialism* and *communism*, two terms which had previously been used interchangeably. Socialism was the first, or lower, stage of the new order. The assumption was that people would still have some of their old prerevolutionary habits. And the economy would not be fully reorganized to provide for unlimited wealth. Therefore, some degree of inequality would remain. People would be paid according to the amount of work they did. The operative slogan was, "From each according to his ability, to each according to his work."

After a relatively short period of socialism (Marx did not say how long), true communism would painlessly evolve. All the means of production (factories, mines, farms, and so on) would be under the control of the people as a whole. The economy would be planned to operate at the highest possible efficiency. New habits of cooperation would replace competition. People would work voluntarily at the jobs they wanted. And as a result all people could have what they wanted. The communist ideal—"from each according to his abilities, to each according to his needs"—would have been achieved.

Engels described his vision of the new order by citing what he believed to be the primitive communism of the Iroquois Indians of North America:

> *Everything runs smoothly without soldiers, gendarmes, or police; without nobles, kings, governors, prefects or judges; without prisons; without trials. All quarrels and disputes are settled by the whole body of those concerned.*[3]

PROBLEMS WITH
THE MARXIST VISION

Of course, Engels's image of Iroquois life was ideal-ized; the reality was much harsher. And there were many other aspects of the Marxist vision that ig-nored inescapable realities. For example, neither Marx nor Engels ever worried about corruption un-der communism. They assumed that corruption, greed, and other vices were the products of oppres-sive social conditions, such as those that existed under capitalism. As soon as good conditions were the norm under communism, most human vices would disappear.

Other people with similar communist ideals were quick to point out some of these problems. Prominent among them was a Russian nobleman named Michael Bakunin (1814–1876). Marx and Bak-unin, who became bitter enemies, differed over the institution of the state (the government, police, law, and the like). Marx believed the proletariat would have to to take over the state and use it to establish the new communist order. Then society could run itself and the state would "wither away." Bakunin argued that the state had to be destroyed first, and that only then could communism be realized. This belief that communism required the immediate and total destruction of the state was called anarchism.

The passage of time has not been kind to either Bakunin's or Marx's vision. No anarchist society of any size has ever successfully been established, and no Marxist society has avoided massive abuses of power by those in control. By contrast, the system of checks and balances embodied in the United States

Constitution has guided an enormously successful, if imperfect, working democracy for over two hundred years. Nor has time borne out Marx's belief that human nature is easily changeable. Change the mode of production and its superstructure, Marx insisted, and human nature will change with it. Establish a wealthy and fair society, and everyone will be content. But today anyone who has studied psychology would find it ridiculous to imagine that good social conditions alone are enough to make everyone happy. Borrowing a word from Marx himself, most people would say it is "utopian" to believe in a society where people get along so well that all work is done voluntarily and there is no need for prisons, judges, or governors.

Another problem is that Marxism was a combination of ingredients that didn't completely blend. One element of that mixture was moral protest against the effect of society, and especially capitalist society, on human beings. Marx believed that capitalism forced most people to struggle just to survive, while socialism would allow the full development of each human being. But this moral protest coexisted uneasily with his claim that he had proved through a scientific study of history that socialism was inevitable.

That study was crucial to Marx and Engels, for it distinguished their "scientific" socialism from the dreams of earlier "utopian" socialists, whom they dismissed as unrealistic dreamers. The problem was that Marx, in his moral protest, began with his conclusion—that socialism *had* to happen—and then proceeded to prove it, at least to himself. After all, Marx and Engels presented their conclusions in 1848 in *The Communist Manifesto,* but Marx did not finish the major work that provided the necessary "evidence"—the first volume of *Capital*—until 1867. By contrast, the scientific method requires the researcher to draw conclusions *after* gathering the necessary evidence. Marx himself never faced that flaw in his methodology. But Engels, just before his death in 1895, indicated that he had an inkling that something might be wrong, since the expected socialist revolution had failed to occur.

MARX AND ENGELS
AFTER 1848

When Marx and Engels wrote *The Communist Manifesto,* they genuinely believed that the "spectre" they said was haunting Europe would become real in their lifetime—that the socialist revolution would occur. The years after 1848 were a bitter disappointment, with socialists and radicals defeated everywhere. In France, the epicenter of the revolution, the upheaval brought the conservative dictator Louis Napoleon to power. In 1864, Marx became involved in founding an international socialist organization called the International Workingmen's Association (later known as the First International). He played a leading role in the organization, but a bitter conflict with Bakunin for control led to its collapse by 1872.

That event closely followed the rise and bloody suppression of the Paris Commune (1870–71), which was the last major radical uprising in Europe during the lifetime of either Marx or Engels. A number of socialist and Marxist parties were founded, most importantly the German Social Democratic Party (SPD, for its German name) in 1875. But despite the

Workers drag a cannon through the streets during the uprising of the Paris Commune. The revolt was crushed.

prominent role of Marxists in the SPD, its program did not meet with the master's approval. Meanwhile, conditions for workers in England and the other capitalist countries of Europe improved instead of worsening as Marx had predicted.

Marx was so disappointed in the developments in Western Europe that he began to toy with the idea of a socialist revolution breaking out in Russia, a backward and largely unindustrialized country. Marx was attracted to a group of Russian socialists (who, ironically, were not Marxists) because they used violent methods at a time when there was so little activity elsewhere in Europe. The Russian socialists were able to assassinate their emperor Alexander II in 1881, but the regime survived.

Two years later, in 1883, Karl Marx died, shortly after the death of his oldest daughter, Jenny. Her death at a young age, coming just a year after his wife's death, broke Marx's heart and seemed to rob him of the will to continue his struggle. The small group that attended Marx's funeral heard Engels deliver a moving eulogy for his friend and collaborator. He began by saying that the world's "greatest living thinker has ceased to think." He paid tribute to Marx's struggle against the evils of capitalism and his passionate struggle for a better, socialist world. Engels also recounted Marx's accomplishments and ended with the prediction that "his name will endure through the ages, and so also his work." [4]

Whether that prediction was accurate or not, it is indisputable that Marx's work had an enormous impact on the twentieth century as a new generation of Marxists picked up the banner of the fallen prophet.

CHAPTER FOUR

LENIN AND BOLSHEVISM

The death of Marx in 1883 and then Engels in 1895 meant that the task of shaping Marxism was passed on to a new generation of revolutionaries. But forces greater than mere individuals were at work remolding Marxist doctrine for the new century. These forces were not the same everywhere; they varied from country to country. As a result, like so many doctrines that began from a common source but changed as they spread, Marxism evolved into different forms, some of which its founders would not easily have recognized.

WESTERN EUROPE

In the late nineteenth and early twentieth centuries, the major forces reshaping Marxism in Western Europe were improving economic conditions for

workers and the growth of parliamentary democracy. Factory workers saw their lives improve for
several reasons. General prosperity brought benefits
to most segments of European society. Workers in
many industries were able to form trade unions and
thereby win higher wages and better working conditions. At the same time, the political systems in
many Western European countries slowly became
more democratic, granting the right to vote to a
growing percentage of the population.

These developments made Western European
Marxists less revolutionary and more reformist. The
workers were far more interested in gradually adding to what they had achieved than in risking all in
a violent revolution for the promise of a miracu-
lously better future. So the intellectuals who led
Marxist movements had little choice but to stress
reform rather than revolution if they were to have
an audience other than themselves. This was especially true in France and England, where Marxism
gradually dissolved into a variety of small groups.

In Germany, the German Social Democratic Party
held together as the largest and most powerful
Marxist party in Europe. It faced special roadblocks:
German laws in force between 1878 and 1890 made
it a crime to advocate socialism or communism. Socialist newspapers were shut down and meetings
banned, and many SPD members fled abroad. But
some activity was still possible, and socialists continued to be elected to the German parliament. With
brilliant leaders like Karl Kautsky (1854–1938), the
SPD's strength grew after the anti-socialism laws were
repealed. The party continued to talk about revolution, but increasingly it worked within the system
for reform. This tendency was reflected on a broader

scale in the international organization of socialist parties called the Second International, formed in 1889. Most of its members became increasingly reformist and less revolutionary with each passing year.

The trend from revolution to reform reached its logical conclusion in the theories of Eduard Bernstein (1850–1932). Bernstein got into trouble with other SPD leaders by pointing out the obvious. Life under capitalism was getting better, not worse. With democratic reforms, violent class struggle was hardly the best way for workers to get what they wanted. Instead, capitalism would gradually and painlessly *evolve* into socialism. Bernstein's theory was given the name "revisionism" because of his revisions of Marx's theories. Many older SPD leaders, including Kautsky, rejected revisionism, at least in theory. But in practice, the SPD operated on this idea.

RUSSIA BEFORE 1900

Meanwhile, Marxism spread eastward to the vastness of Russia, the largest country in the world.

Despite Russia's great size and natural resources, most of its people lived in poverty. Until the 1860s, Russia's peasants, the overwhelming majority of the population, virtually had been slaves, tied to the land either as serfs or, if they lived on state-owned land, as state peasants. By 1900 these people had been free for almost forty years, but that freedom had not liberated most from grinding poverty. While Russia had been industrializing at a rapid pace since the mid-1800s, it still trailed well behind Western Europe. Adding to Russia's troubles, the emperor, or tsar, had virtually absolute power over his subjects.

The interior of the tsar's Winter Palace (top) and the
home of a peasant family (bottom). The life of the
wealthy elite was far removed from the grinding
poverty experienced by most Russians.

Russian society had another major flaw: the gap between its tiny educated elite and the mass of its largely peasant population. These groups rarely interacted and barely knew each other. This would become significant because almost all Russian revolutionaries were from the educated elite, and they thus knew almost nothing about the millions of people they were determined to liberate.

Karl Marx's ideas became known to Russian socialists during the middle of the nineteenth century. The first foreign language translation of *Capital* had been into Russian in the 1870s. In 1883, the same year Marx died, the first Russian Marxist group was formed. Called Liberation of Labor, it was founded by Russian exiles in Switzerland and led by Georgi Plekhanov, a scholarly intellectual whose father was a landowner. But Russia's Marxists were a distinct minority in a socialist tradition already a generation old. Most Russian socialists (who, until the 1880s, were called populists) rejected Marx's view that every nation had to pass through capitalism to get to socialism. The Russians instead believed their country was unique.

The populists believed Russian peasants were socialists by some kind of instinct, having always lived a communistic lifestyle on their *mirs*, or communes. They divided their land equally among themselves and maintained a rough form of equality. These customs actually had nothing to do with socialism; peasant communes existed mainly because the Russian state used them to collect taxes and conscript soldiers for the army. But the populists tended to ignore this historical reality. They believed that if socialists seized power in Russia, the country could be reorganized on the basis of the commune, skip capitalism, and jump directly to socialism.

However, the Russian peasants were illiterate and narrow-minded. They were suspicious of all outsiders, including educated idealists from cities who gave them radical and dangerous advice about overthrowing their tsar. As a result, some populists concluded that educated revolutionaries had to make the revolution by themselves. Acting *for* the peasants, they would seize power, establish a socialist dictatorship, and reorganize the country. No one would be allowed to stand in the revolutionaries' way, including peasants who might disagree with them. While not all populists thought this way, the point of view was held by an important strain of the Russian revolutionary tradition, and it eventually influenced some Russian Marxists.

For over two decades, from the 1860s through the 1880s, the populists attempted and failed to make their revolution. Believing that the end justified the means, some resorted to assassination (including the killing of the tsar in 1881) and other desperate measures. But whatever they tried—from openly appealing to the peasants to organizing secret groups to carry out the revolution or assassinate government officials—they were unable to move the peasantry to follow them. Partly as a result of this failure, some revolutionaries began to turn to a new doctrine imported from Western Europe: Marxism. Marxism explained the populists' failure. It said that the Russian peasantry could never be used to make a socialist revolution. First Russia had to go through capitalism. This would create the modern industry necessary for socialism as well as for creating the class—the proletariat—that would carry out the revolution. Only then could socialist revolutionaries seize power and build the society they wanted.

The debate between Russia's Marxists and populists sharpened during the 1890s. By 1900 both groups were becoming better organized. The Marxists called themselves Social Democrats, the same name Marxists used in Germany, while after 1901 most populists followed a newly organized political party called the Socialist Revolutionaries.

VLADIMIR LENIN AND RUSSIAN MARXISM

In 1870, just before *Capital* was translated into Russian, the man who would change Marxism forever was born in Russia. Vladimir Ulyanov—later to be known as Lenin—was born into a comfortable middle class household in Simbirsk, a provincial town on the Volga River. He later described his childhood fondly:

> We lived in easy circumstances. We did not know hunger or cold, and were surrounded by all sorts of cultural opportunities and stimuli, books, music, and diversions.[1]

When Vladimir was a teenager the happiness of the Ulyanov household was shattered by two blows that hit the family almost simultaneously. In 1886, his father died of a stroke. The next year the family's eldest son, Alexander, was arrested for his involvement in a revolutionary plot to assassinate the tsar. He was executed in 1887, the same year Vladimir graduated from high school at the top of his class.

The next year Vladimir was expelled from his university for participating in a student protest. Eventually he was able to graduate by working at home and taking his exams. More important, he also learned about Russian revolutionary heroes, especially a populist writer named Nicholas Chernyshevsky. Chernyshevsky had written a novel called *What Is to Be Done?* whose main character provided a model of a totally dedicated revolutionary.

During the winter of 1888–89 Vladimir read *Capital*, and by the early 1890s he was a Marxist and once again in trouble with the law. After a term of exile in Siberia, he left Russia for Western Europe in 1900. Now known in the world of revolutionaries as Lenin, he would spend most of the next seventeen years there, shuttling between several European countries. During that period he became one of the most important leaders of Russian Marxism.

Lenin's version of Marxism is so important that it is called, appropriately, *Leninism*. The key point about Leninism is that it combined elements of Marxism with those of the Russian revolutionary tradition. Of course, Lenin considered himself a Marxist and would never have admitted that he changed anything important in the supposedly scientific doctrine of Marx and Engels. And Lenin certainly adhered to Marxism's fundamental doctrines. But he desperately wanted to overthrow capitalism and establish socialism. The problem was that, according to Marxism, Russia still had to pass through most of the capitalist stage of development. Nor could Russia be expected to achieve a socialist revolution until the more industrialized countries of Western Europe had done so. Since historical stages proceed slowly, and since no European country had yet made a socialist revolution, following the traditional Marxist format meant that Lenin would never see the socialist revolution. This was something he could not accept.

Lenin therefore began to tinker with Marxist theory, blending in ideas that helped shorten the time Marxists theoretically had to wait until they could seize power in Russia. His first and most important addition was a new concept of how to organize a political party. By 1900 many Russian Marxists believed that the model should be Germany's Social Democratic party, the SPD—a broadly based organization that permitted a variety of people to join and operated according to democratic principles. But Lenin followed the Russian populist tradition that mistrusted the masses. He insisted that the workers would be satisfied with a few reforms that improved their working and living conditions, but would not see that what was really needed was a socialist revolution. Lenin called this reformist view "trade union consciousness." He warned that if the workers were not directed by someone, the proletariat would never achieve "revolutionary consciousness" and there would never be a socialist revolution. To counter this, Russian Marxists would have to organize what Lenin called a "party of a new type."

Lenin outlined his vision in a pamphlet he published in 1902, called *What Is to Be Done?* in honor of Chernyshevsky's novel. Lenin's organization would be a party of revolutionaries that would take control of the revolution, since the workers could not. It would give them "revolutionary consciousness." The party alone would make the important decisions and tell the workers what to do. Lenin insisted that all party members should be totally dedicated to the cause on a full-time basis. In Lenin's words, they should be "professionals." In addition, the party had to operate in the strictest secrecy, to avoid betrayal to the police. It could not and would not worry about democratic procedures, or, as Lenin called them, the "toys of democracy." Decisions had to be made by the leadership, or *central committee*. The leaders would discuss and debate policy, but once a decision was made everyone was duty-bound to follow it.

In fact, Lenin's "party of a new type" was not new at all. His model for a "professional" revolutionary was taken directly from Chernyshevsky, as Lenin himself freely admitted. His model for the party's organization was taken from the ideas and actual secret underground parties of the Russian populists.

Many of Lenin's fellow Marxists in Russia did not accept his vision for their party, fearing that his "party of a new type," tightly controlled by a central committee, would be dictatorial. The argument over party organization led to a split in the newly organized Russian Social Democratic Party in 1903. The two factions that emerged took names according to which group temporarily was in the majority during a series of votes taken at the meeting where the split took place. Lenin's followers became known as the *Bolsheviks*, a name taken from the Russian word for majority. Those who opposed Lenin were called the *Mensheviks*, from the Russian word for minority. There actually were more Mensheviks than Bolsheviks among the Russian Social Democrats between 1903 and 1912, when the two factions formally broke into separate parties. Outstanding among the Mensheviks was Julius Martov, who before this bitter dispute had been Lenin's close collaborator and friend. But the most devastating criticism of Lenin's ideas came from the pen of a brilliant young revolutionary named Leon Trotsky (1879–1940). In 1904, Trotsky wrote:

> *[Lenin's] methods lead us to this: the party organization first substitutes itself for the party as a whole; then the central committee substitutes itself for the organization; and finally a single "dictator" substitutes himself for the central committee.*;[2]

In later years Trotsky ignored his own warning, joined Lenin and the Bolsheviks, and helped lead them to power. Yet nothing in the thousands of pages he would write ever matched the eerie accuracy of that 1904 sentence. It proved to be a death sentence for many of Lenin's devoted followers, among them Trotsky himself.

Lenin added at least one other critical revision to Marxism. It followed from Marx's analysis that the most economically advanced countries would be the first to overthrow capitalism and begin building socialism. Lenin challenged this assumption. He argued that since Marx's time capitalism had expanded into a worldwide system in which the industrialized countries of Europe exploited the backward nations of Asia and Africa. Lenin called this phenomenon *imperialism* and pointed out that for Russian Marxists it contained both good and bad news. The bad news was that imperialism had delayed the socialist revolution in the industrialized European countries by allowing European capitalists to use some of the wealth they took from Asia and Africa to prop up the standard of living of the European proletariat. The good news, from Lenin's point of view, was that the world capitalist-imperialist system had weak points: capitalist countries that were only partially industrialized. In particular, Lenin pointed out that Russia's capitalist system was extremely unstable because of the country's backwardness and poverty. Therefore, capitalism might collapse first in Russia, and from there the revolution would spread to Europe. This scheme would speed up the arrival of the socialist revolution in Russia and allow Lenin to be there to lead it.

There was one more central element in Leninism: the idea that the end justified the means. This idea, like Lenin's lack of faith in the proletariat, had deep roots in the Russian revolutionary tradition. In the years prior to his party's seizure of power in 1917, Lenin endorsed robbery, fraud, extortion, and many other crimes to further his party's fortunes. After 1917, he showed there was little he would not do to hold on to power. His willingness to go to any length to attain his goals undoubtedly helped bring him to power and keep him there. But it also accustomed Lenin and his followers to acts of cruelty and brutality, which they used to build a society that was supposed to put an end to such things.

Lenin addresses a crowd in 1919. Leon Trotsky,
at first his critic but later his supporter, can
be seen to the right of the podium.

[57]

REVOLUTION: 1905–1917

Despite their best efforts, the Russian revolutionaries could not shake the tsarist regime. Lenin, Martov, Plekhanov, and every other major Marxist leader lived in exile in Western Europe. Then, in 1904, Russia blundered into war with Japan. Russia's tsar, Nicholas II, believed his huge empire would have little trouble defeating the Japanese. He was painfully mistaken. As battle defeats and casualties mounted at the front, so did the hardship at home.

Unbearable conditions eventually led to an upheaval called the Revolution of 1905. The trigger was a massacre of hundreds of peaceful demonstrators—men, women, and children—by the tsar's troops on January 22, 1905, a day that became known as "Bloody Sunday." As the revolution spread from Russia's capital, St. Petersburg, Lenin returned home to lead the Bolsheviks. The star of the revolution, however, was Trotsky. He became the head of an organization of workers in St. Petersburg, called the St. Petersburg Soviet, that led a massive strike against the government. The Soviet was made up of representatives from factories in the capital, and both the Mensheviks and Bolsheviks participated in it.

The Soviet did not survive for long. Neither Lenin's scheming nor Trotsky's heroics were enough to save it once the war ended and the tsar's battle-hardened troops returned home in the fall. By December the revolutionaries were in flight or, like Trotsky, under arrest. It took more than another year to restore order nationwide, but in the end the Revolution of 1905 was crushed.

The Bolsheviks and Mensheviks learned very different lessons from their defeat. Following classic Marxist logic, the Mensheviks concluded that the Russian proletariat was still too small—barely 3 million out of over 140 million—to make a socialist revolution. Only after capitalism had matured and the proletariat was in the majority would the time come.

Lenin and the Bolsheviks saw the matter differently. Lenin's main goal was to strengthen the Bolsheviks so that they could seize power. Unlike the Menshevik leaders, he was unwilling to wait for the proletariat to become the majority. He therefore looked for an ally to increase its numbers. Borrowing yet another idea from the populists, Lenin looked to the peasantry for the solution. If the peasantry became allied to the proletariat, Russian Marxism would be greatly strengthened. Of course, the peasants would not be allowed to decide anything, but if some of their demands were met they could be manipulated into supporting a Bolshevik-led socialist revolution. This idea was terrible Marxism; Marx himself had left no doubt that he thought the peasants were a backward-looking class. But in a country that was overwhelmingly agrarian, Lenin's idea was excellent politics.

Despite the defeat of the revolutionaries, the Revolution of 1905 brought significant changes to Russia. To survive, Nicholas was forced in October 1905 to grant his subjects a constitution and civil rights. Russia now had the first parliament in its history. Called the Duma, it had only limited powers, and voting laws heavily favored the rich and conservative. The government nonetheless undertook some major reforms designed to help raise the standard of living of the peasantry, overhaul the army, and improve educational opportunities for

Russia's children. Russian industry also continued to grow. But the standard of living for most of Nicholas II's subjects remained miserably low, and progressives in Russia's middle and upper classes were unhappy with the limited scope of the reforms. The empire had survived, but its weaknesses left it vulnerable to another shock.

That shock, soon in coming, was World War I, which began in August 1914. It pitted Russia, England, and France against Germany and Austria-Hungary. Each side had several smaller allies, and the United States entered the war on the side of Britain, France, and Russia in 1917. As the war dragged on, Russia suffered many defeats. The effects of war on the home front were far more damaging than the hardships of 1905. In March 1917 demonstrations and riots began in Petrograd, as St. Petersburg had been renamed in 1914. This time nothing could save Nicholas. Within a week he was forced to abdicate and the monarchy itself was abolished. A caretaker government known as the Provisional Government, made up of Duma leaders and moderate notables, took power. A new era had opened up for Russia, and with it new hopes and unforeseen dangers for the country's millions of long-suffering people.

THE BOLSHEVIK REVOLUTION

The moderate and liberal politicians who organized the Provisional Government were committed to establishing a genuine Western-style democracy. They also wanted Russia to keep developing along capitalist lines into a modern industrial society, comparable to England or France. In other words, the Provisional Government stood for reform rather than further revolution. This was reflected in new laws that greatly expanded civil rights and established an eight-hour work day. The Provisional Government also freed all political prisoners and prepared for a national election for a constituent assembly that would give Russia its first real constitution. This basic reformist and democratic outlook did not change even when socialists—mainly Mensheviks and Social Revolutionaries (SRs)—joined the Provisional Government during the following months.

Despite its good intentions, however, the Provisional Government was unable to restore order in Russia. It had trouble controlling the army, especially the garrisons stationed in Petrograd and Moscow. The government was also hampered by socialist-controlled soviets, or councils, that existed in many cities and towns. They were elected directly by those they represented, such as the workers of a city or the soldiers of a garrison, and they often did not listen to the Provisional Government. The most important soviet was in the capital: the Petrograd Soviet of Soldiers' and Workers' Deputies.

The Provisional Government added to its difficulties by staying in the war, which led to enormous casualties. The government also refused to authorize the immediate transfer of all noble land to the peasantry, on the perfectly reasonable grounds that a nationally elected legislature should decide such an important matter. This delay drastically eroded the government's popularity in the countryside, where most Russians lived.

It was into this chaos that Vladimir Lenin boldly and single-mindedly strode when he returned home in April 1917, after years in exile. The March Revolution had taken him by surprise. Only two months earlier he had said that he did not expect to live to see the revolution in Russia, and when the news came, Lenin at first refused to believe it!

The Bolshevik-Menshevik split in the Marxist ranks now became critically important. The Mensheviks' view of Marxism had turned them into a relatively moderate party willing to cooperate with the Provisional Government. The government was working to establish a democratic system, and the Mensheviks were convinced it was important to support that effort for the good of Russia. The fall of the tsar was a giant step forward; the last thing the Mensheviks wanted was a new dictatorship to replace the old one. And the defeat of 1905 had taught them that cooperation with liberal groups was essential if democratic reforms were to succeed in Russia.

Under Lenin's leadership the Bolshevik Party set itself apart from the socialist parties that were cooperating with the Provisional Government. From the very beginning, he was determined to overthrow the Provisional Government and establish a Bolshevik government in its place. Lenin was absolutely convinced that only a Bolshevik dictatorship under his leadership could carry Russia to socialism. Any other course, any compromise with the bourgeoisie or even with other socialist parties, would derail Russia from the socialist path.

Lenin's strategy produced immediate political dividends. The Provisional Government's difficulties and failures discredited all the political parties associated with it, including the SRs and the Mensheviks. In March these two parties had controlled both the Petrograd and Moscow soviets, the most important of Russia's soviets. By the fall, the Bolsheviks were the majority in both bodies.

At this point, Lenin decided the time had come for the party to seize power. His proposal shocked even his closest followers. While some of them may have wanted the Provisional Government replaced, they expected it to be followed by a coalition of all the major socialist parties, not a dictatorship of one party. Lenin had to work hard for a month to convince his central committee to go along with his bold plan. He was helped by a recent recruit to the party, Leon Trotsky, the same man who had criticized Lenin for being dictatorial thirteen years earlier. In October, the central committee voted ten to two to seize power.

Because Lenin was under the threat of arrest and therefore in hiding, most of the organizational work was done under Trotsky's brilliant leadership. During the night of November 6–7, the Bolsheviks struck. The party's armed militia seized key points in Petrograd and arrested most of the ministers of the Provisional Government. The Bolshevik seizure of power went so smoothly that hardly anyone noticed. Most people in the capital slept through it.

It took only twenty-four hours and a few hundred casualties to end Russia's first brief experiment in democracy. In its place began the most important social experiment of the twentieth century: the building of the world's first Marxist and socialist society.

THE BOLSHEVIK
DICTATORSHIP

Under Lenin's decisive leadership, the Bolsheviks, whose control was limited to little more than Petrograd, moved quickly to secure their power. Two decrees issued on November 8 increased the party's popular support. One transferred all of Russia's farmland to the peasants. This was the key part of Lenin's strategy to win peasant support. The second decree announced Russia's desire for immediate negotiations to end World War I. When England, France, the United States, and their allies did not respond, Lenin's government began direct talks with the Germans. The difficult negotiations that followed led to the Treaty of Brest-Litovsk in March 1918. Lenin's government gave up a great deal of territory in exchange for peace, leaving the Western allies to fight Germany alone.

Along with these popular steps, the Bolsheviks moved swiftly to eliminate all their political rivals. The first step was to organize a working government. Lenin again faced opposition among his closest comrades when he proposed that only Bolsheviks be in the government. Several of them frankly warned him that without a coalition of several socialist parties—that is, without some concessions to democracy—the Bolsheviks would have to govern "by means of political terror." The Bolsheviks also were pressured by several independent trade unions and other workers' groups. After much maneuvering, one tiny socialist party was allowed a small voice in the new regime. This arrangement lasted only a few months, after which only Bolsheviks were left in Lenin's government.

Meanwhile, political repression proceeded on other fronts. Newspapers of non-socialist parties were suppressed. Special "revolutionary tribunals" were set up to dispense instant justice, eventually including executions. Russia's largest liberal party saw its members denounced as "enemies of the people." Most important, on December 20, 1917, Lenin's government set up its own secret police, called the *Cheka*. Its job was to repress what the Bolsheviks called "counterrevolution," which in fact meant any opposition to their dictatorship.

In January 1918 the Bolsheviks crushed another rival: the Constituent Assembly. This body had been elected in December 1917 in the first free elections in Russia's history. The election itself had been organized by the Provisional Government several months before it fell, and not even Lenin had dared risk canceling it. As he feared, the Bolsheviks lost the election, finishing a distant second to the SRs. The tumultuous scene at the assembly's first meeting was described by SR leader Victor Chernov, who was chosen its president:

> *I delivered my inauguration address, making vigorous efforts to keep self-control. Every sentence of my speech was met with outcries . . . often buttressed by the brandishing of guns. . . . Tseretelli [a Menshevik leader] rose to answer the Bolsheviks. They tried to "scare" him by leveling a rifle from the gallery and brandishing a gun in front of his face.*[3]

The Constituent Assembly met for only one day before Lenin ordered troops to close it down.

Within months this repression of all political opposition led to civil war. The fighting lasted from mid-1918 until the end of 1920. It was a bitter struggle that pitted virtually every non-Bolshevik political party and faction against Lenin's government. The anti-Bolsheviks, known as the Whites, were helped by several Western governments, particularly Britain, France, and the United States. The Bolsheviks, called the Reds, initially suffered some serious defeats, but they had resources and advantages that finally proved decisive. One critical factor was Lenin's leadership; he kept the party together in the most difficult of times, in contrast to the disunited and often quarreling Whites. Grouped around Lenin were a number of able and ruthless leaders. One was Trotsky, who organized the Bolshevik armed force, known as the Red Army. Another was a Bolshevik from Georgia, a non-Russian country that had been absorbed by the empire during the late 1700s and early 1800s. He was Joseph Djugashvili (1879–1953), a cruel but effective revolutionary who was better known by his underground alias, Stalin.

The Bolsheviks resorted to brutal methods to win the civil war. They established the world's first concentration camps for political prisoners. The *Cheka* hunted down city people hoarding food in order to survive, surrounded peasant villages and shot those who refused to give up their grain, and broke strikes by factory workers. From its modest beginnings as a force of 120, the *Cheka* grew to a huge bureaucracy of 30,000, not including the 125,000 special troops it controlled.

Meanwhile, the Bolshevik government seized all available resources for the war effort. It confiscated food from the peasantry, took control of all factories, banned private trade, and used forced labor for emergency projects. These policies were later given the name War Communism, although at the time they were more of a series of emergency measures than a systematic policy. War Communism destroyed the Russian economy, but it kept the Red Army supplied and was crucial to winning the civil war. After savage fighting, millions of deaths due to cold and starvation, and massive destruction of property, the Bolsheviks won the civil war. The goal of building socialism loomed ahead, but first the Bolsheviks faced the task of repairing a ruined land.

THE NEW
ECONOMIC POLICY

Although the Bolsheviks had won a military victory, their power was not secure. Russia's economy was devastated, leaving millions without adequate food and shelter. There were strikes and riots by workers in the cities and rebellions by peasants in the countryside. A terrible famine that claimed five million lives swept the country during 1921–22.

The most direct threat to Bolshevik power was a rebellion of sailors at the naval base at Kronstadt, an island in the bay just outside Petrograd. The Kronstadt garrison had long been a Bolshevik stronghold; now, however, the sailors demanded an end to the Bolshevik dictatorship, freedom of activity for all socialist parties, and other reforms. In a word, the Kronstadt sailors wanted a socialism based on democracy, not on dictatorship. Unable to persuade their "blinded sailor-comrades" to yield, the

Bolsheviks stormed Kronstadt in a battle worse than any seen during the civil war. One historian described the battle this way:

> *White sheets over their uniforms . . . the Bolsheviks were met by hurricane fire from Kronstadt's bastions. . . . The ice broke under their feet; wave after wave of white-shrouded attackers collapsed into the glacial Valhalla. From three directions fresh columns stumped and fumbled and slipped and crawled over the glassy surface until they too vanished in fire, ice, and water. . . . The bitterness of the attackers mounted accordingly. . . . the Bolsheviks at last succeeded in climbing the walls. When they broke into the fortress, they fell upon the defenders like revengeful furies.*[4]

Thousands died in the battle; thousands more were sent to living deaths in concentration camps. Nor did the end of the battle end the nightmare of Kronstadt. Trotsky and many other Bolsheviks who defended the "tragic necessity" of suppressing Kronstadt were haunted by what they had done for the rest of their lives.

Just before the Kronstadt rebellion began, the Bolsheviks had been meeting in their Tenth Party Congress. The issues before the congress were how to revive the Russian economy and stabilize the party's control over the country. In the wake of Kronstadt, Lenin convinced the congress to abolish War Communism in favor of what he called the New

Economic Policy [NEP]. Its first goal was to end the threat of starvation that hung over Russia. The New Economic Policy ended food seizures and allowed farmers to sell their crops on the open market, paying the government a percentage of their crops as taxes. (Later this was changed to a money tax.) Suddenly, peasants who previously had no reason to plant crops (since the government would take them anyway) had an incentive to grow as much as they could. Within two years, the country had enough food. The NEP also returned small businesses to private hands, while the government kept control of large enterprises like railroads, large factories, and mines. Free trade was legalized. The result was a gradual recovery of the economy by the mid-1920s.

These impressive results nevertheless left many Bolsheviks unhappy. Despite its faults, they had liked the policies of War Communism, which seemed like a major step toward socialism. The NEP, by contrast, was permitting capitalism and inequality, as some people were successful in farming and business and others failed. Prosperous peasants were called *kulaks*, an uncomplimentary term meaning "fists" in Russian. Small traders and businessmen were called *nepmen* and were no more popular with the Bolsheviks than the kulaks.

The NEP created another dilemma. Marxism taught the Bolsheviks that Russia had to build modern industry to become a genuine socialist society. But the NEP was not providing the resources to do this. The state-controlled large industries were not efficient enough to generate the large profits needed for new investment. Nor could the funds be raised by taxing the peasants heavily—the NEP was designed to give the peasants incentives to produce, so the taxes on them were low.

Could Russia industrialize under the NEP, or would it have to find another economic policy? By 1923 this question had become urgent. Lenin and the Bolsheviks had expected that once Marxists seized power in Russia, the revolution would spread to Western Europe. When that happened, it was thought, poor and backward Russia would receive aid from richer and more advanced fellow Marxist countries in the West and would finish industrializing quickly and painlessly. But by 1923 it was becoming clear that there would be no socialist revolutions in Western Europe. This made the question of what the Bolsheviks should do next far more complicated.

POLITICAL DILEMMAS

By the early 1920s the party faced a set of political disputes as well. During the civil war the party leadership increasingly had ignored the wishes of its rank-and-file members. Those who disagreed with the harsh measures used during the struggle against the Whites were silenced. But dissatisfaction with Lenin and the party leadership burst into the open at the same Tenth Party Congress that adopted the moderate NEP economic policies.

The response was anything but moderate. Following Lenin's recommendations, the congress adopted a series of rules that almost completely strangled genuine debate. When dissent continued, the leadership early in 1922 created a new post called the general secretary, one of whose tasks was to help enforce party discipline. Joseph Stalin, on whom Lenin had relied before for difficult assignments, was chosen for the job.

Stalin's selection created more difficulties than it solved. By 1922 Lenin was deeply concerned with a problem he did not expect: corruption within the party. Lenin apparently had been convinced that revolutionaries were uncorruptable. But with no restraints on the party from outside, it is hardly surprising that corruption did develop. Officials used their positions for personal gain. The public, meanwhile, could do little. No free press existed to point out these abuses and urge them to be corrected because the Bolsheviks had suppressed opposition newspapers. Corrupt officials could not be voted out of office because the Bolsheviks had eliminated all rival political parties and abolished free elections.

Lenin was especially worried that his new general secretary, Joseph Stalin, was deeply involved in these abuses. Meanwhile, Stalin was also using his position to accumulate a great deal of power. By the end of 1922 Lenin had decided that Stalin should be replaced as general secretary. Before he could act, however, he suffered the first of three strokes that eventually would kill him. After being bedridden for over a year, he died in January 1924. Control of the party he had founded and the revolution he had so boldly led now passed to a new generation.

LENINISM

Shortly after Lenin's death, the terms Leninism and Marxism-Leninism came into common usage among

Marxists. They referred to the dictatorial form of Marxism that evolved in Russia under Lenin's leadership. It differed greatly from the vision of Marx and Engels, and even more from the moderate view of Marxism that had developed in Western Europe. It therefore is enormously significant that it was Marxism-Leninism rather than any of the more democratic forms of Marxism that came to power, first in Russia and then in other nations.

Leninism was the product of two processes. First, before 1917, Lenin borrowed ideas from the Russian revolutionary tradition that added a clear dictatorial dimension to Marxism. His idea for a "party of a new type," which would control the working class rather than simply lead it, was the most important of these concepts. Second, the merciless struggle for power after 1917 made the party still more dictatorial. Even party members found their rights to speak and influence policy severely limited as maintaining power took precedence over everything else. By Lenin's death, Russia had a new name—the Union of Soviet Socialist Republics—and a new form of government: the modern one-party dictatorial state.

Leninism was so radically different from Marxism as it existed in Western Europe that the two versions parted company completely. The first symbol of that break came when the Bolsheviks changed the name of their party to the Communist Party in 1918. Lenin insisted on the term communism to distinguish his "revolutionary" party from the reformist Marxist parties of Western Europe, which still called themselves "socialist." The second symbol was an organization called the Communist International (Comintern or Third International), which the Bolsheviks set up in 1919. Lenin would have nothing to do with the reformist and democratic socialist parties, including the Marxist ones, of the Second International. The Bolsheviks therefore formed their own international association of communist parties. They were organized in the same centralized and authoritarian way as the Bolsheviks and took their orders from Lenin's party.

Leninism, or Marxism-Leninism, thus was a version of Marxism modified by Russian conditions. It stood not only for socialism, but for the harsh one-party dictatorship the Bolsheviks set up in Russia after 1917. In the generation after its founder's death, Leninism would be further modified by what happened in Russia. Those changes would add yet another significant word to the Marxist vocabulary: Stalinism.

CHAPTER FIVE

MARXISM AND STALINISM

The death of Lenin left the Communist Party of the Soviet Union without the leader who had founded and guided it since its birth. It also left world Marxism without a leading interpreter. The man who filled the first of these two vacancies would also fill the second, because Moscow, the capital of the Soviet Union, was also the world capital of Marxism.

THE STRUGGLE FOR PARTY LEADERSHIP

The two main rivals for leadership were Leon Trotsky and Joseph Stalin. A brilliant theorist, writer, and speaker, Trotsky was by far the better known of the two and the man most observers expected to succeed Lenin. Trotsky's importance in the November 1917 revolution and the civil war was second only to Lenin's. Many observers even referred to the regime as the government of Lenin-Trotsky.

Trotsky was a man of theory as well as action. His most important contribution to Marxism was his theory of "permanent revolution." The theory was close to Lenin's idea that Russia could be the place where the world socialist revolution would begin. According to Trotsky, the revolution that overthrew the tsar would have to begin as the capitalist or "bourgeois" revolution, but it did not have to end that way. Because Russia's capitalist middle class (the bourgeoisie) was just developing and therefore weak, it might immediately be overthrown by the proletariat, which was well organized and working in large modern factories. This action by Russia's small but organized proletariat might then spark a socialist revolution in Western Europe. If the advanced and powerful Western European proletariat came to the aid of Russia's proletariat, Russia could then begin to build a socialist society.

Stalin (the name means "man of steel" in Russian) was cunning and cruel, but also intelligent and able to understand his opponents' strengths and weaknesses. Stalin served Lenin loyally during the endless party disputes before 1917, and during the civil war of 1918–21 he became one of the party's five top leaders. Stalin lacked Trotsky's brilliance as a speaker, writer, and theorist. But he surpassed Trotsky and all other Bolshevik leaders in knowing how to build a political organization. As general secretary, a post no other top leader wanted, Stalin was able to place people loyal to him in key party posts. He also was skilled at building alliances, especially against Trotsky, and then breaking them at

Ruthless and cunning, Joseph Stalin gained
supreme control after Lenin's death.

the best moment for himself. In this way Stalin defeated first Trotsky and then the other top party leaders—a faction led by Grigori Zinoviev (1883–1936) and Lev Kamenev (1883–1936), and finally a group led by Nikolai Bukharin (1888–1938). By 1929 Stalin was in control.

Although not known as a theorist, Stalin was responsible for an important addition to Marxist doctrine during the 1920s: the concept of "socialism in one country." Prior to this time, Marxist theory assumed that socialist revolutions would spread quickly from one country to another. However, by the mid-1920s only Russia had experienced a socialist revolution, and there was little hope of revolution elsewhere, especially in Western Europe. In the traditional theory, the failure of socialism in Western Europe meant the future of socialism in Russia was bleak. By contrast, "socialism in one country" suggested that Russia could build socialism alone. This was exactly what many Bolsheviks wanted to hear, and it helped Stalin win allies in his successful campaign for power. Trotsky was not only denied power but was expelled from the Communist Party and driven from the Soviet Union into exile for the rest of his life.

THE "SECOND" BOLSHEVIK REVOLUTION

What has been called the "Second Bolshevik Revolution," or the "Stalin Revolution," followed Stalin's rise to power. It was the world's first comprehensive attempt to turn a country into a modern industrial state in a very short period of time. True to Marxist concepts, the Soviet economy was to be planned by party and government officials. The Soviet government had a good jumping off point, since in 1929 it already controlled the Soviet Union's mines, railroads, banks, and large factories. But it still had to take control of many smaller industries. Far more important and difficult, the Soviet regime was determined to take control of about 20 million small peasant farms. This would allow it to control the country's food supply.

As significant as the scope and scale of industrialization was the speed at which Stalin and the party leadership wanted it completed. Stalin set a period of ten years to accomplish what in Western Europe had taken a century or more. His official excuse was that there was little time because the Soviet Union was threatened by unfriendly capitalist powers. As Stalin put it in 1931:

> To slacken the tempo would mean falling behind. And those who fall behind get beaten. . . . One feature of the history of old Russia was the continual beatings she suffered because of her backwardness. She was beaten by the Mongol khans. She was beaten by the Turkish beys. She was beaten by the Swedish feudal lords. She was beaten by the Polish and Lithuanian gentry. She was beaten by the British and French capitalists. All beat her—because of her backwardness. . . . They beat her because to do so was profitable and could be done with impunity. . . .

We are fifty or a hundred years behind the advanced countries. We must make good this distance in ten years. Either we do it, or we shall be crushed. [1]

It is impossible to know how much Stalin believed his dire warning. The truth is that the Soviet Union faced no military threats when he made that speech. The most likely cause of the reckless tempo of building that Stalin imposed was his fanatical desire to guarantee his place in history as a great Russian and Marxist leader. It was an expensive wish that would cost millions of Soviet citizens dearly.

THE FIVE-YEAR PLAN

After 1928 the Soviet economy entered a six-decade-long era when its economy was controlled by a series of five-year plans. The First Five-Year Plan, over one thousand pages long, was officially adopted in April 1929. It called for unprecedented leaps in production. In a scant five years, industry as a whole was to grow by 250 percent, while heavy industry—mining, steel production, electricity, machine building, and the like—was to jump by 330 percent. Somehow output of goods for consumers and agricultural production was to rise as well. Making matters even more difficult, the plan was declared to have begun in October 1928, half a year before it was adopted. Stalin later demanded that the plan be fulfilled in four years instead of five.

The plan also required a policy called the "collectivization" of agriculture. The Soviet Union's peasant farms, most of which were small, inefficient, and unable to use modern technology, would be abolished. In their place would be large collective farms. All the land, tools, and equipment from the former peasant farms would be turned over to these new collectives. Their large fields would be ideally suited for using modern machinery and other agricultural techniques. This would increase crop yields, which would make food available to the millions of new industrial workers the plan called for in the cities. Crops could also be exported in exchange for the modern machinery the Soviet Union needed to industrialize.

In theory, and according to official pronouncements, the collective farms would be under the control of the people living and working on them. In fact, they were under the tight control of the Communist Party, and the farmers had little choice but to do what they were told.

The collectivization campaign began late in 1929 and ran into trouble immediately. It was carried out so quickly that it produced chaos and disorganization. In addition, the peasants bitterly resisted the seizure of their farms. The clash between the peasants, armed with farm tools and an occasional rifle, and Soviet government police and soldiers, with an arsenal of machine guns and other weapons, was as one-sided as it was bloody. The slaughter was worse than anything ever seen in the troubled Russian countryside. Villages were surrounded and their people massacred if they resisted. The following account describes what typically occurred:

In 1930 . . . thousands of peasants armed with hunting rifles, axes, and pitchforks

> revolted against the regime. . . . For three
> days . . . a bloody battle was waged be-
> tween the revolting peasants and the au-
> thorities. . . . The revolt was cruelly pun-
> ished. Thousands of peasants, workers,
> soldiers, and officials paid for the attempt
> with their lives, while the supporters were
> deported to concentration camps. . . . Mass
> executions were carried out. . . . The soil
> of this region was soaked in blood. After
> the executions, these villages were set on
> fire.[2]

Adding to the disaster of collectivization was the campaign against the kulaks, the prosperous farmers. They were excluded from the collective farms because they were considered enemies of the new socialist order. Millions of men, women, and children were driven into exile in remote areas of the Soviet Union or sent to the country's growing network of slave labor camps. The death toll of this campaign—called "dekulakization"—reached into the millions. It grew even higher when a deadly famine struck the Ukraine and several other parts of the Soviet Union in 1932–33. The main cause of this famine was the government's seizure of almost every available scrap of food. The crops went to feed workers in the cities and for export, while the peasants who had grown them starved. The Stalin regime used the famine to break resistance to collectivization in areas like the Ukraine where opposition was especially strong. Stalin called his policy "war by starvation." A survivor described what he saw as a thirteen-year-old boy:

The peasants ate dogs, horses, and rotten
potatoes, the bark of trees, grass—any-
thing they could find. Incidents of canni-
balism were not uncommon. . . . And no
matter what they did, they went on dying,
dying, dying.

They died singly and in families. They
died everywhere—in yards, in streetcars,
and on trains. There was no way to bury
these victims of the Stalinist famine. [3]

The Stalin regime crushed peasant resistance, but only at great cost. Peasants killed their farm animals and destroyed their tools rather than surrender them. Half the Soviet Union's horses, almost half its cows, and about two thirds of its sheep were lost, some because of peasant resistance and others because of mismanagement by communist officials who knew nothing about agriculture. Food production dropped by 20 percent and did not reach 1928 levels until the start of World War II. In 1953, the year Stalin died, grain production was less than in 1913.

One reason for this was constant interference in farming operations by government officials who worked in distant offices rather than on the farms themselves. Stalin's government refused to provide the resources—from farming supplies to decent storage facilities and adequate rural roads—necessary for successful farming. Perhaps the most important reason for low production was that collectivized peasants made poor workers. They worked on two types of farms: the *kolkhoz* and *sovkhoz*. A *kolkhoz*, or collective farm, officially was owned and managed by its members. In reality, these farms were

Workers harvest grain on a collective farm in the Ukraine.

run by the party. A *sovkhoz*, or state farm, officially was run by the government; its farmers were paid a straight wage. Whichever farm the peasants worked on, they were paid very little. So they worked very little, and carelessly when they did. Most of their efforts went into tiny private plots they were allowed to tend. Amounting to about 3 percent of the Soviet Union's farmland, these plots produced at least a third of the country's fruit, milk, meat, eggs, and vegetables. Overall, Marxist agriculture in the Soviet Union was a colossal failure.

Almost all of the country's resources, including those taken from the peasants, went into the campaign to build heavy industry. During the 1930s the Soviet Union built a vast array of mines, mills, factories, power stations, and dams designed to match the industrial and military might of the advanced capitalist nations. This overwhelming emphasis on heavy industry left almost nothing for the production of consumer goods such as housing and clothing. The frantic pace of construction often resulted in bottlenecks and breakdowns, which wasted huge amounts of scarce resources. There was no excuse for not meeting Stalin's impossible targets. Managers and other officials often paid for shortfalls with long prison sentences.

The gigantic glamour projects Stalin ordered, including dams, canals, and huge industrial works, produced more waste. An observer remarked that Stalin seemed to want "a canal that could be seen from Mars." One candidate for that honor—the Baltic–White Sea canal, built at reckless speed at the cost of 250,000 lives—proved useless because it was too shallow.

Despite unyielding pressure, almost none of the targets of the first two plans were met. In fact, the plans themselves were little more than propaganda statements. Real planning was limited to one or, at most, two years. Some targets were reached as the result of crash campaigns in which selected projects received priority. Frequently, in the mad rush to reach a particular goal, quality was ignored. The required tonnage of a certain steel would be produced, but it would be unsuited for the machine or building project for which it was intended. Some shoes or clothing might be produced, but they would fit badly and fall apart almost immediately.

What few consumer goods were available were distributed unequally. The Communist Party leadership received good apartments, ample supplies of food, and many luxuries, while ordinary Soviet workers and peasants often did without the bare necessities of civilized life.

Nonetheless, the achievements of the first two plans were impressive, at least in terms of Stalin's goals. In barely eight years, Soviet steel production rose from 4 to 17 million tons. Oil jumped from 11.7 to 30.5 million tons, and coal and electricity by similar amounts. The automobile, tractor, and chemical industries were created from scratch. Heavy industry grew overall by 400 percent. A modern industrial base was built. But the cost was millions of lives, enormous waste, and social upheaval. During the 1930s, the Soviet Union experienced the greatest peacetime decline in a country's standard of living in history. Stalin achieved much of what he had wanted, but he did not deliver what Marxism had promised.

THE GREAT PURGE

Between 1934 and 1938, Stalin carried out a campaign of arrests, murders, and banishments unprecedented in scope, cruelty, and destructiveness. Almost all the party leaders who had participated in the Bolshevik Revolution were accused of unbelievable crimes and executed. Hundreds of thousands of loyal party members met similar fates. Millions of ordinary Soviet citizens were arrested and sent to labor camps, where many were worked to death. Three fourths of the party leadership as of 1934 were shot, as were thousands of the Red Army's best officers. No less than 8 million people died in this Great Purge, and the toll may have been much higher.

Purges were nothing new in the history of the Communist Party. Lenin had carried them out, and Stalin had expanded on them during the late 1920s and early 1930s. But neither the Communist Party nor the Soviet Union had ever seen anything like Stalin's Great Purge. It brought fear and terror to almost every corner of Soviet life. It killed millions of people who were perfectly obedient Soviet citizens. It crippled the Soviet military and disrupted the economy. It swept through the party like an unstoppable plague and spread even through the ranks of the secret police who were carrying it out. Its deadly crowning highlight was a series of three show trials of former Bolshevik leaders, one each in 1936, 1937, and 1938. Among the defendants were the best of Lenin's comrades, including Zinoviev, Kamenev, and Bukharin. All these hardened revolutionaries confessed to crimes against the revolution they could not have possibly committed—a testimony to the mental and physical tortures perfected by Stalin's secret police. Then, in late 1938, the Great Purge ended as suddenly as it had begun. A last echo of its deadly thunder, however, was heard in 1940 when Leon Trotsky, living in exile in Mexico, was murdered by one of Stalin's agents.

"Why? What for?" were the questions that thousands of terrified and mystified victims scratched on their prison walls. The answer lies buried with Stalin, who never gave a reason for this rampage. The most likely explanation is that Stalin carried out the purge to give himself absolute power. Prior to 1934, Stalin exercised dictatorial power, but he had to depend on the support of other powerful party leaders to do so. The Great Purge and its reign of terror gave Stalin the absolute power he craved by eliminating any possible challengers in the party and leaving most Soviet citizens so frightened that their main concern was to stay out of trouble.

As if to prove his power, Stalin had himself glorified as the greatest man alive. The Soviet propaganda machine pictured him as the man responsible for virtually every Soviet accomplishment since the revolution. Cities, towns, streets, and other public places were named for Stalin; paintings and statues of him were everywhere. A typical schoolchildren's song thanked Stalin "for the sun Thou has lit." This "cult of Stalin," as critics later called it, was further evidence of how completely one man controlled a revolution that was made, in theory, to give power to the people.

TOTALITARIANISM

Marxism had promised equality and freedom and more. Under communism, society would be so fair and run so smoothly that government and its tools of repression—what Marxists called the state—would be unnecessary and disappear.

Under Lenin and especially under Stalin, the reality was totally different. The state did not wither away. Instead, it grew and grew, becoming so powerful and overwhelming that it dwarfed any state that had come before it, even the powerful Russian autocracy. Under Stalin it had such power to control society that it gave rise to a new category of government: the totalitarian state. The Soviet totalitarian state controlled almost all aspects of life in the Soviet Union. Following Marxist doctrine, it ran the economy: the country's factories, farms, transportation network, shops, and services. All educational institutions, sports clubs, and newspapers took orders from the state. Even artists and their creative works fell under state control. According to Stalin, art should deliver messages that contributed to the building of socialism. Artists who dared to defy the Soviet regime found themselves unable to work or, worse, in labor camps where many of them died.

Soviet citizens could not travel abroad without permission. They even needed passports to travel *inside* the country. The state constantly spied on the people, and it maintained the world's largest secret police to make sure the job was done thoroughly. Government spies lurked in factories, apartment houses, schools, and almost anywhere else people gathered.

The state itself was controlled by the only legal political party: the Communist Party of the Soviet Union (CPSU). Every level of government was run by party personnel, so much so that Western observers described the Soviet regime as a "party-state." The Soviet Union was not the world's only totalitarian state after 1930. Nazi Germany was one in the 1930s and 1940s, as was the People's Republic of China after 1949. But no totalitarian regime controlled its people's lives more thoroughly than Stalin's regime in the Soviet Union.

All this made a mockery of the Marxist vision of the state withering away under socialism. This did not bother Stalin, who simply changed Marxist theory to suit his needs. To explain why the Soviet state was growing stronger rather than weaker, Stalin proclaimed that internal and external enemies made this necessary. Since nobody in the Soviet Union dared disagree with him, Stalin's explanation became part of Soviet Marxist doctrine.

Why did Marxism lead to a totalitarian system in Russia? Or, in other words, how did Marxism turn into Stalinism? The answer must begin with Marxism itself. Marx believed that the checks and balances so important in democratic societies, such as the United States, were unnecessary in a socialist world. Once the proletariat took over, it would not be corrupted by power because the old evils that had once caused this would be gone. The assumption that the new system would automatically regulate itself was basic to Marx's thinking. It proved to be a tragic misconception.

Leninism also contributed to the development of totalitarianism, by justifying a one-party dictatorship. Once all opposition parties, the free press, and all other forms of organized opposition to state power were eliminated, the road to totalitarianism was open. In addition, both Marx's and Lenin's ideas justified state control of the entire economy of a country. This added enormously to the state's power, which increased even further when the Bolsheviks undertook rapid industrialization under state control.

The influence of tsarism had made the Russian soil fertile ground for totalitarianism. Russia had a centuries-long tradition of state control over a passive population. The Bolsheviks were treading on firm political ground when they assumed their government could act without considering the people's desires. Of course, the Bolsheviks went much further and did much more than any tsar. This was because of their determination to completely overhaul Russia and build a socialist society. They also went further because twentieth-century technology allowed them to. The type of control the Soviet regime exercised would have been impossible without modern communications and other advances that simply were unavailable to earlier dictatorships.

Finally, there was the character of Stalin himself. He played a critical role in selecting and enforcing policies that built the Soviet totalitarian state. The great terror of the 1930s, which completed the building of that state, was Stalin's work. To be sure, it was not his work alone, any more than Nazism and the Holocaust were solely Hitler's work. Both tyrants were able to realize their horrible plans because large numbers of people cooperated and participated in their heinous crimes, some reluctantly and others enthusiastically. But just as it is difficult to picture a Bolshevik Revolution without Lenin, or Nazism and the Holocaust without Hitler, it is virtually impossible to picture the extreme brutality of industrialization and collectivization, as well as the great terror, without Stalin. And that is why after Stalin's death the totalitarian system he built slowly began to erode.

EASTERN EUROPE

One of the reasons Stalin ended the great terror was the growing threat presented by the rise of Nazi Germany. That threat exploded into war in June 1941, when Germany invaded the Soviet Union and brought the horrors of World War II deep inside Soviet territory. The Soviet Union and its communist system barely survived World War II, and not only because of German military power. Millions of Soviet citizens hated communism and greeted the German invaders as liberators. They soon found out that the invading Nazis brought with them not liberation but more killing and oppression. Assisted by the United States and other countries also fighting Germany, the Soviet people rallied behind their leaders to drive the Germans from their country. The cost of the war was enormous. At least 20 million Soviet citizens died, and large parts of their country were left in ruins.

Prior to World War II, the only other communist state in the world besides the Soviet Union was the People's Republic of Mongolia, set up in 1924 when the Soviet Union helped drive Chinese forces from the region. World War II dramatically changed that situation. The major Soviet gain from World War II was the spread of its power and its version of Marxism into Eastern Europe. After the Red Army drove the Germans from Soviet soil, it also pushed them out of Eastern Europe. Between 1945 and 1948, with the Red Army occupying much of the region, the Soviet Union set up puppet communist regimes in Poland, Romania, Bulgaria, Hungary, and Czechoslovakia. Local communist movements, meanwhile, seized control of Yugoslavia and Albania. In 1949, the Soviet Union also set up a communist dictatorship in its occupation zone in Germany, creating the Democratic Republic of Germany (East Germany).

Communism in Eastern Europe increased the power of the Soviet Union, which for the first time controlled a large chunk of Europe outside its own borders. Eastern Europe provided the Soviet Union with a buffer zone against the influences of the capitalist West. It also was proof to the Soviet leadership that communism was advancing in the world. But with the exception of those in Albania and Yugoslavia, none of these regimes could have survived long on their own. They were organized under Soviet control and kept in power by Red Army occupation troops or large Soviet forces close to their borders. Several times—in 1953 in East Germany, 1956 in Hungary, and 1968 in Czechoslovakia—it took Soviet tanks to prop up communism.

No communist propaganda could hide the fact that all of the regimes of Eastern Europe except Yugoslavia and Albania were Soviet puppets. Often they were called the Soviet bloc or Soviet "satellites," a reference to their lack of real independence. Nor could propaganda negate the fact that the standard of living in communist Eastern Europe was much lower than in capitalist Western Europe. Maintaining communism in Eastern Europe became one of the prime objectives of Soviet policy. It was the single most important cause of the Cold War, the forty-five-year-long era of tension between the Soviet Union and its communist satellites and the United States and its capitalist allies. The Cold War divided Europe into two military alliances: the U.S.-led North Atlantic Treaty Organization (NATO), organized in 1949, and the Soviet-dominated Warsaw Pact, set up in 1955. It also produced the most expensive and dangerous arms race in history, a huge buildup of nuclear arms that for decades left the entire world teetering on the brink of nuclear war.

Despite the spread of Soviet power, the immediate post-war era gave the Soviet people no rest. The economic sacrifices continued as Stalin's regime focused on heavy industry. Purges and arbitrary arrests also continued. When Stalin finally died in March 1953, the Soviet Union was the world's number two industrial and military power, trailing only the United States. But millions of Soviet citizens still were in labor camps, and most of those who were free lived in wretched poverty, as the full weight of totalitarian Marxism bore down on them.

CHAPTER SIX

SOVIET MARXISM AFTER STALIN

The decade after Stalin's death was a search for balance. Stalin's successors knew that life could not continue as it was before 1953. The secret police terror that had left nobody safe, from the top party leaders to ordinary citizens, had to be ended. The miserably low Soviet standard of living had to be raised. Otherwise, only continued terror could keep the Soviet people under control. The problem was that there was little agreement about how far to go in reforming the system Stalin had left behind. In addition, several men were competing to succeed Stalin as the Soviet Union's leader.

Despite these difficulties, a few reforms were made almost immediately. Before the end of 1953, the power of the secret police was broken. Its chief, a sinister Stalin henchman named Lavrenti Beria, was arrested, tried, and shot, and the organization became an instrument of the entire party leadership, as it had been before Stalin's rise to power. In the future it would be used only to protect the Communist regime, not to maintain a terroristic personal dictatorship. The Soviet Union still did not have freedom as that term is understood in the West, but people at least could be reasonably sure that if they followed the rules they were safe from arrest.

Meanwhile, a limited attempt was made to increase food supplies and consumer goods for the long-suffering Soviet people. For the first time in years, party leaders made public statements about the need to raise the standard of living. The new Soviet leadership also took steps to reduce tensions with the United States and its allies.

Gradually one of the lesser known of the party's inner circle, a tough man of peasant origin named Nikita Khrushchev, emerged as the top Soviet leader. Khrushchev never had nor wanted Stalin's dictatorial power. In fact, one of the few areas of agreement among Stalin's successors was that none of them would ever be allowed to become a tyrant like him.

The new leader of the world's most powerful Marxist country and party, and therefore of world Marxism, did not seem suited for the job. He was not a scholar like Marx or a brilliant revolutionary like Lenin. The men he worked with considered him reliable but crude, a man of limited ability. But in the end Khrushchev surprised almost everybody. He not only saw the need for greater reforms than most of his rivals advocated, but was daring and courageous enough to try new policies.

Khrushchev faced several major obstacles in undertaking reform. Because he was not a dictator like Stalin, he could not introduce reforms before lining up support among the party leadership. Khrushchev also faced the dilemma of how much reform to introduce. The great worry among the party leadership was that one reform could lead to another too quickly and then run out of control. Perhaps most important, Khrushchev had to battle Stalin's legend, which still was very much alive. His rivals could always appeal to Stalin's memory in arguing against changes Khrushchev wanted to make.

These obstacles forced Khrushchev to undermine Stalin's authority and to revise some of the accepted notions of Soviet Marxism. Khrushchev did this in an unsystematic and erratic way. He never challenged any of Marx's assumptions, nor did he write theoretical works as Lenin and Stalin had done. But in his speeches and, far more important, in his actions, Khrushchev challenged both Stalin and Lenin. In the process, he improved the conditions in his country and softened the hard face of Soviet Marxism.

KHRUSHCHEV
AND REFORM

By the time Stalin died, the Soviet version of Marxism had three great prophets: Marx, Lenin, and Stalin. Khrushchev dramatically changed that lineup by removing Stalin from the group. He took on Stalin directly on the night of February 25, 1956, just as the 20th Party Congress of the CPSU was about to close, in a four-and-a-half-hour "secret speech" to the party delegates. The speech shocked not only the delegates but the rest of the Marxist world when its contents became widely known.

Nikita Khrushchev waves to a crowd while touring France in 1960. The Soviet leader attempted to smooth relations with the West.

Stalin, whose propaganda machine had made him almost a god in the communist world, was exposed as a leader with terrible flaws. Khrushchev denounced his former boss as a tyrant who had murdered thousands of loyal communists.

> Lenin used severe methods only in the most necessary cases . . . Stalin, on the other hand, used extreme methods and mass repressions at a time when the revolution was already victorious. . . . It is clear that here Stalin showed in a whole series of cases his intolerance, his brutality, and his abuse of power. . . . He often chose the path of repression and physical annihilation, not only against enemies, but also against individuals who had not committed any crimes against the Party and the Soviet government.[1]

Khrushchev's revelations were incomplete, to say the least. He said nothing about Stalin's and the party's crimes against millions of Soviet peasants and workers during collectivization and the industrialization drive. Nor were millions of non-party victims of the labor camps mentioned. But what Khrushchev did say was enough to throw the communist world from Eastern Europe to East Asia into turmoil. His remarks also shattered the faith of many Marxists outside the communist world. They helped clear the path for reform in the Soviet Union, but also caused instability that almost led to Khrushchev's fall from power.

The process of reducing Stalin's reputation was called *destalinization*, and it quickly led to violent disturbances. The most serious difficulties were in the satellites of Eastern Europe, where resentment against communism combined with the yearning for independence from Russian control. In Poland, riots and strikes brought a faction of reform-minded communists to power. The new leadership was still communist and loyal to the Soviet Union, but it demanded the right to introduce some policies different from those followed in Moscow. Khrushchev accepted these changes only when he realized that he would have to use military force to stop them.

In Hungary there was far less room to maneuver. As in Poland, local discontent brought several reformist communists to power. But Hungary's longstanding hatred for Russia boiled over into open revolt against communism and foreign domination. It took Soviet tanks and thousands of deaths to restore order and communist control.

In 1957, Khrushchev himself faced a challenge from his rivals at home, who used the events in Eastern Europe to try to remove him. Khrushchev beat back their challenge and then turned his victory into a major reform. Since 1953, with the exception of Beria's execution, Soviet power struggles had avoided bloodshed. Khrushchev now confirmed this change: His defeated rivals were sent into retirement, and in fact given comfortable pensions for the rest of their lives.

Khrushchev meanwhile made a major change in Soviet Marxism by modifying his country's foreign policy. At the same party congress where he made his secret speech, the delegates passed a resolution calling for "peaceful coexistence" between the communist and capitalist worlds. Ever since Lenin, the Soviets had proclaimed that capitalism and communism could not coexist, that their differences eventually would have to be settled by war. Khrushchev found this unacceptable. He knew that by the 1950s such a war would be fought with nuclear weapons, and that it could have no winner. He therefore rejected war as an option, and said that the competition between the two systems would be peaceful. The winner would be the system that provided its citizens with a better life and standard of living.

Khrushchev believed that communism would win that competition. After 1956 he devoted the bulk of his time and energy to raising the Soviet standard of living to assure the triumph of communism. Some of his efforts were successful, especially his program to build more housing. But Khrushchev's attempts to improve Soviet farming had mixed results. Under a project called the virgin lands program, begun in 1954, millions of acres in Soviet Central Asia were brought under the plow. Khrushchev hoped this would permit a dramatic increase in food supplies at very low cost. This program produced some good harvests, but it also ran into serious problems. By the 1960s, this region, which had not been farmed before because of limited and erratic rainfall, was swept by drought and disastrous dust storms.

One of Khrushchev's most important insights was his realization that no reforms could be completely successful unless the people as a whole enthusiastically supported them. He therefore worked tirelessly touring the country, urging ordinary Soviet citizens to support his efforts. He also reduced censorship, allowing writers and artists far more freedom. He hoped greater freedom of expression would win the educated elite to his side.

The great paradox in this was that while Khrushchev wanted the people involved in what *he* decided to do, he was unwilling to let them decide on policy. That power would remain strictly with the Communist Party and its leadership. Still, Khrushchev tried to emphasize that the government was paying more attention to the people by making another change in Marxist doctrine. In 1961, he announced that instead of a dictatorship of the proletariat, the Soviet Union had evolved into what he called a "state of the whole people" and that the Communist Party had become a "party of the whole people." Of course, changing a few definitions did nothing to change who ran things in the Soviet Union. This fact was not lost on the millions of average Soviet citizens.

THE END OF KHRUSHCHEV'S REFORMS

The reform program was plagued with other problems. Khrushchev was impatient and sought results quickly and cheaply, often at the expense of the planning and investment it took to do the job right. The virgin lands project was one example of this. Another was a reorganization of the planning system introduced in 1957. Khrushchev hoped to move some of the important decisionmaking from Moscow to the various regions of the country, so economic decisions would be made by people who knew local conditions. But his reform caused a great deal of confusion and waste, and it threatened the jobs of top officials in Moscow. These officials therefore resented Khrushchev, who found himself making powerful enemies within the party. Other enemies were in the military, which opposed Khrushchev's attempt to reduce the military budget in favor of civilian economic needs. Khrushchev turned still more officials against him when he began to reorganize the Communist Party late in 1962. By then many of his former supporters had become disillusioned with him.

Foreign policy problems added to his difficulties at home. His attempt to improve relations with the United States did not meet unanimous approval in the communist world. But, ironically, it was a conflict with the United States that did the most to undermine Khrushchev. During October 1962, the world's two leading nuclear powers came dangerously close to war in what became known as the Cuban Missile Crisis. The crisis developed when the Soviets tried to install nuclear missiles in Cuba, which by 1962 was a communist state and Soviet ally. The United States demanded the missiles be withdrawn and threatened to go to war over the issue. The Soviets were forced to back down because of overwhelming U.S. military superiority, a retreat that infuriated the Soviet military and many other party leaders.

Khrushchev never fully recovered from the crisis. In October 1964, after months of secret plotting, the party leadership united against him and removed him from power. He was voted out of office by the party's Politburo, its top decisionmaking body.

The legacy of Khrushchev's years in office was mixed. His policies ended Stalin's terror, led to the release of millions of innocent prisoners, and raised the Soviet standard of living. His support of scientific research enabled the Soviet Union to score many important firsts, including the world's first artificial satellite and the first man in space. Relations with the West improved, and a partial ban on nuclear testing was signed in 1963. The very fact that he could be voted out of office without violence was a major improvement on the past, as Khrushchev himself pointed out.

The Soviet Union was still a rigidly controlled society, dominated by a single dictatorial political party. The inefficient centrally planned economy was basically unchanged. Overall, however, Khrushchev brought about needed and overdue change. His fall meant that the process of reform was stopped. This would have grave consequences for the Soviet Union and Marxist regimes that followed its example.

BREZHNEV AND STAGNATION

Replacing Khrushchev was a leadership team headed by Leonid Brezhnev, a long-time supporter who had deserted Khrushchev at the end. Brezhnev would remain in power for eighteen years, longer than any Soviet leader except Stalin, until he died in 1982. Like Khrushchev, Brezhnev was not a dictator. He was the most powerful of a small group of leaders who controlled the Communist Party. That leadership in turn represented the interests of party officials who did the day-to-day work of controlling the Soviet Union. In a sense, by the 1960s the Soviet Union was an oligarchy, ruled by a small but well organized group. Brezhnev's job was to preserve that rule by avoiding any changes that would threaten stability, and he did it for almost two decades.

Brezhnev began by reversing some of Khrushchev's most radical policies, including his economic decentralization program and his reorganization of the Communist Party. He also ended Khrushchev's destalinization policies, and even partially restored Stalin's reputation. Since stability at home meant safety abroad, Brezhnev tried to limit tensions with the United States. These efforts included a major arms control treaty in 1972, the first since the start of the Cold War.

But maintaining stability at all costs proved to have a high price. There were many people in Soviet society who wanted Khrushchev's reforms continued. Prominent among them were many educated people who expected further reductions in censorship and state control. They were angered and disappointed when Brezhnev reversed Khrushchev's reforms in this area. Some of them secretly began to turn against the communist system, while a few especially courageous people did so openly. Among the latter was Andrei Sakharov, the Soviet Union's leading nuclear scientist. In 1968 he wrote an open letter to the Soviet leadership. Called "Thoughts on Progress, Peaceful Coexistence, and Intellectual Freedom," it warned that "freedom is essential to human society" and that the failure to continue reforms toward freedom would cripple the Soviet Union and turn it into a second-rate power. Sakharov was persecuted and eventually put under house arrest.

The same year that Sakharov published his letter, the Brezhnev regime issued its own statement about the future. The so-called Brezhnev Doctrine stated bluntly that the Soviet Union would use force to prevent any communist bloc country from reverting to capitalism. By claiming that socialism could not be reversed under any circumstances, the Brezhnev regime made its only significant contribution to the evolution of Marxist theory.

Neither the house arrest of Sakharov nor the threat of the Brezhnev Doctrine did anything to solve the growing problems in the Soviet Union. By the 1970s the country increasingly was plagued by protests by non-Russian ethnic minorities. The movement that received the most attention was the campaign by Soviet Jews, who had endured centuries of anti-Semitism under both the tsars and the Soviets, to emigrate from the Soviet Union and go to Israel. However, other ethnic minorities and religious groups also were restive.

At the same time, the Soviet economy was running into trouble as the inefficiency of central planning stifled attempts to modernize the economy. Military spending drained vital resources from other needs. As growing numbers of Soviet citizens saw their lives fail to improve, they sought ways to escape their problems. Social problems such as alcohol abuse grew worse. When Brezhnev died in 1982, the Soviet Union was on the brink of a crisis.

CHAPTER SEVEN

CHINESE MARXISM AND MAOISM

After World War II, Marxism had two great flagships: the Union of Soviet Socialist Republics and the People's Republic of China (PRC). While over a dozen smaller communist ships of state steamed behind in their deep and wide wake, it was these two Marxist giants that determined both the direction and stability of world Marxism. But the Soviet Union and China were not always effective leaders, nor did they always pull in the same direction.

The Chinese are an ancient people whose civilization stretches back over four thousand years. China first was unified over two thousand years ago; for centuries at a time, under several different dynasties, it was one of the world's most powerful and technologically advanced empires. But by the middle of the nineteenth century, China had fallen on hard times. Plagued by overpopulation and growing poverty, its civilization and the government that rested on it were in decay. Weakened by its internal problems and unable to match the modern technology of the West, China was falling prey to European colonial expansion. These problems eventually developed into the worst crisis China had ever faced.

As a result of the so-called Opium Wars of the 1840s and 1850s, several European powers led by Great Britain began to interfere in China's internal affairs. The British even took over a small area in southern China that included the city of Hong Kong. The Manchus, the ruling dynasty that had come to power in the seventeenth century, barely survived an enormous rebellion that tore through the country between 1850 and 1864.

The decline of China drew the attention of Karl Marx. Marx believed that the civilizations of Asia had developed differently from those of Europe. Beginning with slavery, Europe had evolved through feudalism and capitalism. China and India, Marx wrote, were based on another system, the "Asiatic mode of production." This was characterized by self-sufficient villages and an extremely powerful central government. The key point, according to Marx (who knew more about India than China), was that the Asiatic mode of production was static. It did not evolve like the economic systems of Europe. Marx therefore stressed that his analysis of historical change applied only to Europe, *not* to Asia.

The only possibility of change in China and India, Marx said, was from outside forces. He therefore supported the spread of European colonialism to India and China, a view that his followers today find embarrassing. Capitalism, introduced into Asia, would destroy the Asiatic mode of production. This would open the road to socialism and a better life for all. Or, as Marx put it in defending British colonialism in India:

> *England, it is true . . . was actuated only by the vilest interests, and was stupid in her manner of enforcing them. But that is not the question. The question is, can mankind fulfill its destiny without a fundamental revolution in the social state of Asia? If not, whatever may have been the crimes of England she was the unconscious tool of history in bringing about the revolution.*[1]

By the 1890s, the threat that China would be divided up by several European colonial powers and Japan was real. In 1894–95, China was defeated in a war by Japan, which then annexed some Chinese territory, including the island of Formosa. A few years later several European powers took direct control of some parts of China, mainly along the coast. Legally these territories were "leased," but these "leases" seemed to be the first step toward China's division.

The Chinese, especially the educated elite, were dejected and demoralized. By the turn of the century, many educated Chinese began to turn to new ideas they learned from the Westerners whose power seemed so overwhelming. They decided China needed a revolution to overthrow the Manchus and establish a Western-type government in its place. When the Manchu dynasty collapsed in 1911, these

Western-influenced intellectuals got a chance to use their new ideas to solve their country's problems.

China's revolutionaries made up only a minuscule percentage of a population that was well over 90 percent peasant and largely illiterate. In the years after 1911 they proved unable to establish an effective government. In fact, after 1916 the country sank into anarchy, and local strongmen called warlords ruled in China rather than a central government.

The outstanding Chinese revolutionary leader was a man named Sun Yatsen, who headed a political party called the Nationalist Party, or Guomindang (GMD). Most of Sun's ideas were drawn from the West. Their core was what he called the "Three People's Principles": nationalism, democracy, and a vague version of socialism he called the "people's livelihood." While Sun's ideas contained some ambiguities, he basically wanted China to follow the path of the Western democracies. He managed to get himself designated "president" of China but had no power to pull the divided country together. He strengthened his government and the Guomindang after 1923 when he reached an agreement for aid with the Soviet Union. Before he could begin reunifying China, however, Sun Yatsen died of cancer in 1925. He was succeeded as GMD head by a young military officer named Chiang Kaishek.

MARXISM IN CHINA

Marxism came to China in the aftermath of World War I, as a result of two crucial events. The first was the victory of Bolshevism in Russia and the proof of its ability to set up a strong central government to begin building socialism. The second event occurred in China in 1919. China had supported the Allies in their struggle against Germany during World War I. As a result, the Chinese expected German-controlled areas in China to return to Chinese control after the war. Instead, the Western democracies allowed the Japanese to take over those territories. This infuriated millions of Chinese. The day the decision was announced in China—May 4, 1919—enormous riots took place. A small group of Chinese intellectuals became disillusioned with the Western democracies and began to look elsewhere for the solution to China's problems. They found their answers in Marxism and Leninism and in the Communist Party of the Soviet Union.

The Chinese Communist Party (CCP) was organized with Russian help in 1921. Its two main leaders were Chen Duxiu and Li Dazhao. The idea of a Marxist party in China was in some ways far-fetched. Capitalism and modern industry had a foothold only in the foreign-controlled areas. The Chinese working class was tiny, a few million out of perhaps half a *billion* people. But the example of Bolshevism was crucial. Marxism had been applied in Russia, a backward country, with what at the time seemed like remarkable success. So after 1917 communist parties began to spring up in several non-industrial countries, including China.

Like all of the world's communist parties, the CCP took its orders from Moscow. In 1923 those orders were to form a temporary alliance with the Guomindang. The Soviets calculated that a Guomindang-CCP alliance—or "United Front"—would be able to unify China and force the Western European powers out. Unable to exploit China, the European capitalists would grow weaker. This would bring the socialist revolution closer in Western Europe, which is what the Soviets wanted.

The United Front strategy was followed between 1923 and 1927. Some CCP leaders were unhappy with it. They did not trust Chiang Kaishek, who had a reputation as a militant anti-communist. These concerns turned out to be valid. In 1927, in the middle of a military campaign to unify China, Chiang suddenly turned on the CCP. Thousands of its members were murdered. Chiang's sudden assault obviously brought an end to the United Front; it nearly ended the CCP as well. A few lucky CCP members managed to escape Chiang's forces and flee into the remote countryside, where they rethought their strategy and began to rebuild their party. Among them was Mao Zedong.

MAO ZEDONG AND CHINESE MARXISM

Mao Zedong was born in 1893. His father was a prosperous peasant; by the standards of China's hard-pressed peasantry, he was considered wealthy. The eldest of four children and strong-willed, Mao did not get along with his father and defied him by attending primary school in his determination to get an education. Later Mao participated in the revolution of 1911 and then attended a teacher-training school. But he did not become a Marxist until after 1918, when he went to Beijing. There he was influenced by Li Dazhao, who was in charge of the library at Beijing University, where Mao worked. In 1921, Mao Zedong, a Marxist for barely a year, became one of the founders of the CCP.

Mao Zedong became the guiding force of Chinese Marxism. In this historic photograph he proclaims the establishment of the People's Republic of China in 1949.

After the disaster of 1927, Mao found refuge in a remote mountain region in southern China, where he began rebuilding an organization. The basis of this work, however, was radically different from European Marxist thought. Mao adapted Marxism to fit the conditions in China. His central point was that a revolution in China would have to be based on the *peasantry*, not the proletariat. From a traditional Marxist point of view this made no sense; it was, in fact, heresy to say that the peasantry, which Marx had dismissed as ignorant and politically hopeless, could carry out the revolution. Yet Mao stated his view with great force:

> *In a very short time . . . several hundred million peasants will rise like a mighty storm, like a hurricane, a force so extraordinarily swift and violent that no power, however great, will be able to suppress it. They will smash all trammels that bind them and rush forward along the road to liberation.*[2]

Party leaders who outranked Mao and continued to take orders from Moscow did not agree with his ideas. But Mao and his followers, isolated in their mountain stronghold, usually were beyond the reach of orders from the Soviet Union or CCP leaders.

Mao was determined that the CCP would never be helpless again, as it had been in 1927. He therefore focused on building an army that could protect the party as it worked to win supporters. At the same time, the army was trained to treat the civilian population well. Mao stressed that the CCP was the weaker force in its conflict with the GMD and had to have the support of the people. Thus, unlike war-lord or GMD armies, the CCP army never abused the peasants or stole from them. Its conduct helped the CCP win friends and attract recruits.

Mao meanwhile added another concept to his version of Marxism—the importance of human will, an idea he seems to have picked up from Li Dazhao. Mao believed that with the proper will revolution-aries could overcome any obstacle. Here Mao again was playing fast and loose with Marxism. Accord-ing to Marx, early twentieth-century China was not ready for socialism. It lacked industry and the pro-letariat. According to Mao, these deficiencies did not matter, as long as there were peasants and revolu-tionaries with the proper will.

Against all odds, Mao's efforts in southern China were remarkably successful, at least for a while. By 1931 he was strong enough to declare an "indepen-dent" state he called the Chinese Soviet Republic. Of course, that state was surrounded by the Repub-lic of China, which was run by a Guomindang dic-tatorship headed by Chiang Kaishek. But within the narrow borders of the Chinese Soviet Republic, Mao and his followers ruled. They did not rule gently. They seized the property of landlords, using force when necessary, and gave it to poor peasants. Mao also used his army against his rivals within the party. One dispute ended in thousands of arrests, mass trials of Mao's opponents, and the execution of several of them. Meanwhile, Chiang Kaishek made several at-tempts to destroy Mao's regime. In 1934, on his fifth try, Chiang's army, equipped with modern weapons and advisers from Nazi Germany, crushed the com-munists and drove them from their bases.

Mao and his comrades once again barely escaped with their lives. They fled southern China with Chiang's forces in hot pursuit in a chase that lasted a full year. This desperate escape is known as the Long March. In barely a year it covered over 6,000 miles (10,000 kilometers). It finally ended in 1935 with what was left of the communist forces—100,000 started the Long March and only 10,000 finished— in a desolate province in northeastern China. Now, for the first time, Mao became the official leader of the party. In 1936 he set up his new headquarters in the town of Yanan, and once again started to rebuild.

THE YANAN WAY

The CCP under Mao's leadership had barely set up shop in Yanan when, in 1937, Japan launched a full-scale invasion of China. Although World War II did not officially begin until the German invasion of Poland in 1939, the war began for China with this attack. The Japanese quickly overran China's coastal cities and most of its richer areas, including the Yangtse River valley. They conducted the war with extraordinary brutality, killing millions of Chinese. The war had a devastating effect on the GMD government, which was forced to retreat into China's interior, far from its former areas of support and revenue. The CCP and GMD found themselves pressured to bury their hatchet and sign a "Second United Front" agreement to fight the Japanese. More of an uneasy armed truce than anything else, the Second United Front saw its two partners fighting each other as much as they fought the Japanese.

It was in Yanan during World War II that Mao further developed the strategy that had been evolving before 1934 into a winning formula. The "Yanan Way," as it was called, had several crucial parts. One was called the "mass line." This meant that the party could not simply tell the peasants what to do. If it was going to make a socialist revolution, party workers (who were called cadres) had to live with the people and learn to understand their problems. They had to listen as well as speak, and share the peasants' hardships. Only then could the party successfully lead the peasantry. The "mass line" was not a democratic idea; the party, not the peasantry, was to make the important decisions. But by following the mass line, Mao believed, the party would respect the peasantry and be able to respond to its needs, while it led the peasants toward the party's chosen goal of socialism.

Another crucial part of the Yanan Way was a system of tough control called *zhengfeng*. *Zhengfeng* had both practical and theoretical aspects. On the practical side, intensive training of this sort helped create cadres who were reliable and dedicated. This strengthened the CCP immeasurably. On the theoretical side, Mao's stress on thought control grew out of his ideas about human will. If human will was decisive in the struggle for revolution, it was essential that cadres have the correct frame of mind. Thought control was a crucial tool to make sure that the party stayed on the right path.

Nationalism also was an important part of the Yanan Way. During World War II the CCP often worked behind Japanese lines and engaged in guerrilla warfare against the occupiers, mobilizing millions of Chinese in the struggle against Japan. This cost many lives, but it won the CCP a reputation as a patriotic organization that was not afraid to stand up for China against a powerful foreign invader.

The Yanan years saw one other important addition to Chinese communism: the cult of Mao Zedong. Mao was raised to the status of a near superman, much as Stalin had been in the Soviet Union. This began as a result of the Long March, which Mao and his supporters used to portray him as an invincible leader. By 1942, party workers were hard at work studying Mao's writings. The next year Mao was made chairman of the party. In 1945, the new CCP constitution contained specific references to his ideas, which were called the "Thought of Mao Zedong." No other party leader was so honored. By 1949 a typical song praising Mao called him not only the "Great Hero Mao" but the "Great Savior of the People." After the CCP came to power in China, the cult of Mao became even more exaggerated.

By the time the Japanese were defeated in 1945, communist strength had grown immensely. The CCP controlled hundreds of thousands of square miles and about 90 million people. It was far more popular than the GMD, whose government was known for its corruption. Within a year of the end of World War II, China was torn by a civil war between the CCP and GMD. Although the GMD won several early victories with the help of American aid, by 1949 the communists had swept them from all of mainland China. The Guomindang retreated to Formosa (Taiwan), where it survived behind the naval and air shield of the United States. On the mainland, the CCP set about the task of building its version of a Marxist socialist society.

BUILDING SOCIALISM

The CCP spent the next three years consolidating its power and repairing the damage done by years of war. It instituted a land reform program that divided the land of China's landlords among millions of poor peasants. It decreed a marriage reform law that gave women legal equality with men. It also expanded its apparatus and organized government agencies to control the huge territory and population of China. The party leadership carried out these policies quickly and efficiently, but with ruthless brutality. The army and secret police crushed any opponents, among them several million landlords.

Beginning in 1953, the party turned to building socialism with its First Five-Year Plan and the collectivization of agriculture. Collectivization was carried out far differently than in the Soviet Union, whose disastrous experience the CCP did not want to repeat. Peasants were collectivized in stages, beginning with limited forms of cooperation and ending several years later with collective farms. Calling on its years of experience working among the peasantry, the CCP at first relied on persuasion and incentives to convince peasants to join the collectives. If these tactics did not work, the CCP did not hesitate to use violence, including execution, against peasants who resisted. However, the CCP did not repeat Stalin's wholesale campaign of expulsion and murder against the more prosperous peasants, which so crippled Soviet agriculture. In China those peasants were allowed to join the collectives.

The party's policies were successful. By 1957, over 90 percent of China's peasants were collectivized. However, the first signs of what eventually became a bitter division in the CCP already had appeared. Many peasants resisted collectivization, especially as it approached its final stage, when they had to give up their land. There were also many problems in organizing collective farms, mainly because party members lacked the training and skills to manage them. Some moderate party leaders urged that collectivization be slowed down until these problems could be overcome. This group was led by Liu Shaoqi, a Long March veteran with a distinguished record as a party leader. Mao bitterly opposed any slowdown, insisting that sufficient will power could overcome any problems. Those who wanted to slow the pace, he complained, were "tottering like women with bound feet, constantly complaining that others are going too fast." [3] In the end the process was finished at Mao's pace but with concessions to the peasants, who were allowed to keep small private plots and a few farm animals.

A similar difference of opinion developed over the Five-Year Plan. The plan followed the highly centralized Soviet model, the only example of planned economic and industrial development under socialism available to the CCP. Party planners drew up targets for economic growth, stressing the expansion of heavy industry. Thus steel, coal, electricity, and other industries grew rapidly. But agriculture grew very slowly; in fact, grain production failed to keep pace with population growth. Mao complained that agriculture and the peasants were being neglected. He also disliked the Soviet approach, which allowed the central planners and bureaucrats to decide everything. It violated his Yanan-style "mass line," and in Mao's opinion created the danger that a CCP separated from the masses would become a new ruling class in China. And if a new ruling class evolved, Mao warned, it would mean the restoration of capitalism.

THE GREAT LEAP FORWARD

These and other concerns led Mao Zedong to a grandiose new strategy called the Great Leap Forward. As the name suggests, Mao hoped that China could leap from its first experiments with socialism directly to communism. His strategy was based on the belief that if the party could tap the revolutionary enthusiasm of hundreds of millions of Chinese, it could accomplish miracles. China would be able to raise dramatically both industrial and agricultural production, while *at the same time* achieving communist-style equality. Mao used physics to illustrate his point:

> *Our nation is like an atom. . . . When this atom's nucleus is smashed the thermal energy released will have really tremendous power. We will be able to do things we could not do before.*[4]

The institution that was the real springboard for the Great Leap was known as the people's commune.

Within a few months, over 500 million Chinese peasants were herded into about twenty-six thousand of these communes. The average commune contained about 25,000 people, farmed an average of 100,000 acres, and contained over 100,000 farm animals. To insure equality, people were paid the same regardless of the work they did. Private plots were abolished. Families ate in huge mess halls to free millions of women from their kitchens for labor in the fields. Work went on at a feverish pace, continuing as "voluntary" work after hours. Millions of peasants were mobilized into work gangs and sent far from their home villages to labor on major projects such as dams and irrigation canals.

Peasants also were told to build factories on their communes so industry and agriculture could develop together. The famous symbols of this program were the so-called "backyard furnaces." These were crude homemade structures where millions of peasants, workers, students, and others devoted their free time to making steel. All of China seemed to be hypnotized by Mao's promise that they could expect "hard work for three years, happiness for a thousand." A steel-making campaign in one rural county was typical of what engulfed China:

> *Furnace fields were everywhere. . . . From a distance the leaping flames and columns of smoke look like some new construction site accidentally ablaze. On the scene the atmosphere is like a fairground, with scores of people bursting in and out of the rows of furnaces . . . Small red flags*

*fly overhead indicating the sections be-
longing to the various companies and
squads of farmer-steelworkers who are organized like militia units. The air is filled
with the high-pitched melodies of local
operas pouring through an amplifier above
the site and accompanied by the hum of
blowers, the panting of gasoline engines,
the honking of heavily laden lorries, and
the bellowing of oxen hauling ore and
coal.*[5]

No enthusiasm, no devotion, no songs or flags could
save the Great Leap. The people's communes were
a disastrous failure. Equal pay regardless of the work
performed resulted in many people shirking their
responsibilities. Peasants were angered when they
were drafted to work in distant places. They were
demoralized by regimentation and overwork, and
infuriated by the inefficient mess halls in which they
were forced to eat. The gigantic communes quickly
turned into a management nightmare. And the highly
publicized backyard furnaces, which consumed
scarce resources and wore out their overworked op-
erators, produced useless steel. They stood as proof
that it took advanced technology and careful planning, not revolutionary enthusiasm, to make steel.

The Great Leap Forward actually lurched the
country's economy backward, with disastrous de-
clines in food production and industrial output. The
situation was so bad that Mao was removed from
his post as president of the PRC, although he re-
tained his more important post as party chairman.
His replacement as PRC president was Liu Shaoqi.

Liu headed a team of moderates that included Deng Xiaoping, a tough veteran of the Long March, and Chen Yun, the party's leading economist. Under Liu's leadership the party reversed most of the Great Leap Forward policies. The people's communes, while not officially disbanded, were broken down into "production teams" that corresponded to the old collective farms. Peasants again were allowed to farm small private plots and sell what they raised in rural markets. Within three years China's economy had recovered. But those years, which the Chinese still call the "three bitter years," were a nightmare in which China endured what probably was the worst famine in human history. No less than 20 million people died, and perhaps many more.

In the wake of the Great Leap, the split in the CCP between the Mao and Liu factions became too wide to cover up. It was known as the "Red versus Expert" debate. "Red" referred to the idealism and ideological purity that Mao demanded. All policies had to be what he defined as "socialist." He therefore opposed private plots and material incentives such as high wages for skilled people, insisting they could only lead to capitalism. Mao also believed that building communism depended on loyalty to pure communist ideology rather than on skills or expertise. The "Experts," led by Liu, disagreed. They argued that a tiny private plot on a socialist collective farm did not undermine socialism, but simply made it work better. They also said that expertise and skills were essential to building a modern, industrial socialist society. Because of the disastrous Great Leap, Liu's faction set most economic policies in China into the mid-1960s.

THE SINO-SOVIET SPLIT

The Great Leap contributed to another dispute that was several years in the making: the quarrel between the PRC and the Soviet Union. Relations between Soviet and Chinese communists had never been good. The help and advice the CCP received from the Soviet Union from the 1920s through 1949 had been minimal. At times, such as the days of the First United Front, Soviet advice led to disaster. Mao had risen to power in the CCP by ignoring Soviet advice, and Stalin and Mao neither liked nor trusted each other. However, as long as Stalin lived he was the undisputed head of world Marxism, and Mao had to recognize him as such.

After Stalin's death in 1953, the gap between the Soviets and Chinese began to grow. Mao clearly considered himself the equal of any Soviet as a Marxist leader, and in fact felt his credentials as a Marxist revolutionary exceeded theirs. Mao strongly disapproved of Khrushchev's destalinization speech. He worried that it might destabilize international communism, and he knew that Khrushchev's criticism of Stalin's "personality cult" could be applied to the cult of Mao in China. Mao also strongly disapproved of Khrushchev's attempts to raise the Soviet standard of living. To Mao this pandering to material needs smacked of "capitalist" methods and influences. He also bitterly opposed Khrushchev's attempt to improve relations with the West. Finally, as a Chinese patriot, Mao resented Russian annexations of Chinese territory in the nineteenth century.

Khrushchev had his own complaints about Mao and the CCP. He considered the Soviet Union to be the leader of world communism, and himself to be the world's leading communist. Khrushchev thought the Great Leap was a crackpot idea, and he made fun of it. The Soviet leader also was irritated by Mao's attitude toward the West and the United States. Khrushchev believed that in the nuclear age it was essential to avoid a war that could destroy all civilized life. He was appalled when, in 1957, Mao stated that even if a nuclear war wiped out half the world's people, that would be tolerable because imperialism would be destroyed.

The Sino-Soviet split boiled over in 1960 when Khrushchev suddenly withdrew all Soviet aid from China. In 1962, Mao denounced Khrushchev for backing down in the Cuban Missile Crisis. The next year the Chinese condemned the Soviet Union for signing a partial nuclear test ban treaty with the United States and Great Britain. Mao rejected what he called Khrushchev's "phony communism."

Nor did matters improve after Khrushchev's fall from power in 1964. In 1965 Mao warned that the new Soviet leadership was restoring capitalism. In 1969, the two communist giants fought several bloody battles along their tense border. The unity of the world communist movement had been shattered beyond repair.

THE CULTURAL REVOLUTION

The culmination of Mao Zedong's struggle to find a satisfactory road to communism was the Cultural Revolution of 1966–69. Mao's return to power after the Great Leap disaster was aided by several loyal supporters. Most important was Lin Biao, China's defense minister, who turned the People's Liberation Army into a powerful base of support for Mao. In 1965, the PLA published a small red volume called *Quotations of Chairman Mao*. Soon there were tens of millions of this "Little Red Book" in print. To the uncounted millions who read its short extracts from Mao's writings and waved the book high in the air, it was the source of the wisest ideas in the world. Another important supporter was Jiang Qing, Mao's fourth wife. A former actress, Jiang was totally devoted to her husband, and especially to the violent and fanatical ideas he advocated during the Cultural Revolution.

The Cultural Revolution was based on Mao's belief that the CCP under Liu had become corrupt and was following policies that would lead to the restoration of capitalism. By 1966, aided by the PLA, Mao was prepared to take any measures necessary to push Liu and his supporters out of power.

Aside from the PLA, Mao's main instrument in his battle against Liu and the other party "Experts" was a newly created organization called the Red Guards. The Red Guards were teenage students who generally had not been successful in China's highly competitive schools and who therefore had little chance of attending a university and achieving a high position in society. Membership in the Red Guards enabled them to vent their frustrations and attack the system that seemed to deny them the opportunity to advance. Eventually more than 11 million youths joined the Red Guards. Their guiding light was Mao, who now more than ever was raised to the status of demigod. As one newspaper put it:

Chinese students march in 1965, bearing a poster of Karl Marx and copies of Mao's "Little Red Book."

*Sailing the seas depends on the helms-
man, the growth of everything depends on
the sun, and the making of revolution depends on Mao Zedong's thought. . . .
Chairman Mao is the reddest sun of our
hearts.*[6]

Spurred on by Mao's urging to "bomb the headquarters," the Red Guards swarmed all over China
attacking what they called the "four olds": old
thought, old customs, old culture, and old habits.
Party officials, teachers, professors, intellectuals, and
anyone who tried to stop their rampages became their
victims. Often these people were brutally beaten in
public rallies attended by as many as 100,000 people. Many died from their wounds. The Red Guards
attacked anything foreign, burning Western books,
destroying musical instruments and paintings, and
beating, torturing, and killing intellectuals they accused of being influenced by foreign ideas. Not even
foreign diplomats were safe.

Nor did the Red Guards spare China's own historical treasures. They tore through China's mu-
seums, leaving priceless works of art and invaluable
archaeological finds smashed to bits in their frenzy
to "smash the old; build the new."

Violence not seen since the civil war of the
1940s engulfed China, from its major cities to deep
into the countryside. There were bloody fights when
peasants and workers trying to protect their farms
and factories resisted the Red Guards. And when
there was nobody else to fight, different gangs of Red
Guards turned against each other, with each group

claiming to be the most "radical" and therefore the only group true to the teachings of Chairman Mao. An eyewitness to the fighting in the provincial city of Changsha in central China, who was a teenager at the time, described what he saw in 1967:

> That summer, things got worse in Changsha: The rebels began fighting among themselves. Those who had once been comrades became mortal enemies, and the streets of Changsha ran with blood in the hundred-degree August heat. . . . A civil war was going on, with each side claiming to love Chairman Mao better than the other, to be protecting his revolutionary line against the policies that threatened it. Both sides were willing to die for the right to wield power under Chairman Mao's name. . . .
> It was absolutely terrifying. Bullets whistled in the streets. . . . The city shook with explosions and gunfire, and at night the sky flashed light and then dark with the passing of rockets.[7]

Meanwhile, Mao's wife Jiang Qing led a campaign to overhaul Chinese culture and replace it with what was called a "proletarian" culture. This meant banning most plays, operas, ballets, and other forms of entertainment, whether Western or Chinese. They were replaced by works that had what Jiang believed were proper revolutionary themes, which meant mainly workers and peasants overcoming their oppressors. Chinese artists who were unable to produce what Jiang demanded lost their positions and were unable to work.

The Cultural Revolution soon brought such chaos to China that Mao, his party opponents defeated, drew back. The Red Guards were sent home, and by 1969 order was restored. But China had paid a heavy price. Hundreds of thousands of people were dead. Millions of careers lay in ruins. The economy was disrupted; industrial production dropped disastrously. China's relations with foreign nations suffered.

One area of Chinese life that was devastated by the Cultural Revolution was education. Schools had been closed; when they finally reopened, the old educational standards were abolished. Political correctness, which meant loyalty to Mao's ideas, became more important than academic achievement. As a result, an entire generation of Chinese students received an inferior education. It became known as the "lost generation."

Once the violence was ended in 1969, Mao and his followers ran China until the chairman's death in 1976. They continued many of the same policies, although in less extreme forms, that they had followed between 1966 and 1969. However, Mao soon found himself at odds with Lin Biao, his defense minister and one-time devoted supporter. Disagreements over policy and Lin's efforts to position himself as Mao's successor led Lin to attempt a coup against Mao in 1971. It ended with Lin's death.

Meanwhile, Mao found that to repair the damage of 1966–69 and counter the influence of the army, he needed the help of the experienced people he had purged and persecuted during those years. Liu Shaoqi had died in prison from cruel treatment in 1969. But Deng Xiaoping, a strong supporter of Liu's, was restored to a leadership position in 1973. He was joined by thousands of like-minded party officials. In other words, the need to govern China in an orderly fashion forced Mao to bring back the very people he had so recently accused of betraying his communist ideals.

When Mao died in September 1976, only a few months after the death of his long-time associate Zhou Enlai, the CCP was almost evenly divided between supporters and opponents of the Cultural Revolution. The two sides agreed on only one thing: They feared the fanatical Jiang Qing—and with good reason, since Jiang was planning a coup to seize power. In October, just before she could launch her coup, Jiang and her associates were arrested. She and her three closest allies, nicknamed the "Gang of Four," were sent to prison.

A struggle for power then began between Deng and his supporters and Hua Gofeng, the man Mao had chosen as his successor. By the end of 1978, Deng was firmly in control.

CHAPTER EIGHT

THE FRINGES OF MARXISM

Although the Soviet Union and the People's Republic of China were the world's leading Marxist powers, after World War II Marxists took control of a number of other countries in Europe, Asia, Africa, and Latin America. In some cases—in Eastern Europe and in North Korea—these regimes owed their establishment and continued existence to the presence of the Soviet Red Army. In other cases—including Cuba, Ethiopia, Vietnam, and Cambodia—local Marxist forces came to power on their own, although often with Soviet or Chinese help. All of the Marxist parties that managed to come to power were part of the Marxist-Leninist tradition, which by the 1960s included both pro-Soviet and pro-Chinese groups. The period of Marxist expansion lasted from the 1940s through the 1970s.

EASTERN EUROPE

Most of the regimes in Eastern Europe owed their existence to Soviet military power and therefore had to follow the Soviet model of communism until Stalin's death in 1953. However, once the Khrushchev reforms began, change came to Eastern Europe as well, and several of the Soviet satellites introduced policies different from those in the Soviet Union. Although all reforms and changes took place under the stern, watchful eye of Moscow, some local variations of the Soviet communist model evolved.

The only country to modify the Soviet model while Stalin lived was Yugoslavia, which under the leadership of Joseph Broz Tito broke away from Soviet control in 1948. Before then, Tito had considered himself a loyal supporter of Stalin. However, Tito's communist movement had come to power on its own after World War II, after bitter fighting with non-communist political forces. They also had significant public support, having fought vigorously against the German occupiers of Yugoslavia during World War II. Once in power, Tito fought with Stalin—mainly because Stalin wanted Tito and Yugoslavia under his control, while Tito considered himself an ally but not a puppet. As a result, Yugoslavia broke from the communist bloc, accepted aid from the West, and became neutral in the Cold War.

Tito followed more moderate economic policies than Stalin and in effect created a new communist model. Farms were decollectivized and small businesses were allowed to operate. Workers' councils in factories were given a role in management decisions, and there was more cultural freedom.

However, Yugoslavian communism had plenty of problems. Its political system remained under Tito's autocratic control. He cut short the careers of any talented politicians who might one day challenge him. He did nothing to lessen hostilities between Yugoslavia's various nationalities, including the bitterly hostile Serbs and Croats. Eventually, even Yugoslavia's pioneering economic reforms ran into trouble. Valuable resources were wasted as Tito's dictatorship became increasingly corrupt. By the time he died in 1980, after ruling Yugoslavia with an iron hand for thirty-six years, Yugoslavia was in decline.

The other Eastern European experiments in modifying Soviet communism were even more limited than Yugoslavia's, mainly because the countries involved were part of the Soviet bloc. In the late 1960s, the Hungarian leadership installed by the Soviet Union in 1956 began a policy of economic reform called the New Economic Mechanism. These reforms limited central planning to long-range goals and gave factories more freedom to make their own decisions. About half of all prices were decided by market forces. However, these limited reforms could not solve the basic problems of an economy run by an inefficient and corrupt one-party dictatorship.

The boldest reform attempt in the Soviet bloc was made in Czechoslovakia. In 1968, a group of reformers led by Alexander Dubcek took control of the Czechoslovak Communist Party. The new leadership announced that it intended to establish what it called "socialism with a human face" and proposed genuine democratic reforms, including secret election of party leaders, limited terms for those

A student waves a national flag from atop a Soviet
  tank during the 1968 invasion of Czechoslovakia.
  The invasion succeeded in snuffing out a reform
  movement there.

leaders, and an end of censorship. This new period of hope—which might have provided a model for change in other communist states, including the Soviet Union—was called the Prague Spring. However, the Soviet leadership feared that Dubcek's reforms would undermine communist control of Czechoslovakia and, if allowed to spread, would become a threat to communist power in the Soviet Union. Late in August 1968, the Soviet Union led an invasion of over 500,000 Warsaw Pact troops into Czechoslovakia. Dubcek and his followers were removed from office, and a hard-line leadership was placed in control. For the next twenty years, that harsh dictatorship ruled Czechoslovakia.

Twelve years later Soviet communism faced another serious challenge, this time in Poland. The challenge came from people outside the party who wanted to get rid of the system, not reform it. The ordinary people of Poland—workers, farmers, intellectuals, and others—were fed up with poor living conditions, a corrupt communist leadership, and continued Soviet control. When the government raised food prices in July 1980, a series of strikes broke out. In August, in the industrial port city of Gdansk, workers at the Lenin Shipyards defied the communist regime by forming a trade union. Unlike the officially recognized trade unions in Poland, the new union was controlled by its members, not the communist regime. Called Solidarity, the union was headed by a former electrician named Lech Walesa, who quickly showed he was a skilled and tough leader. Because Solidarity enjoyed almost unanimous support among Poland's people, the Communist regime was forced to deal with it. On August

31, the government signed a historic agreement with Solidarity. It became the first independent union in the communist bloc and the first to be recognized as such by a communist government.

Solidarity's existence clearly was a challenge to absolute communist control of Poland, something the Soviet leadership recognized. The Soviets were also afraid that what they called the "Polish disease" would spread, even to the Soviet Union itself. They therefore pressured the Polish communist leadership to undermine Solidarity. On the night of December 12–13, 1981, after a year of tension, the government struck. It proclaimed martial law, arrested Solidarity's leaders, and dissolved the union.

But the communist regime could not govern. The communists were widely hated in Poland, and the people did nothing to help the government. The Polish economy, already in shambles from decades of communist mismanagement and corruption, continued to decline. In effect, there was a stalemate between the people, who could not get rid of their government, and the government, which could not solve the country's growing problems.

The other countries in Eastern Europe, whether under direct Soviet control or not, were harsh Stalinist dictatorships. The regime in East Germany, the country with the strongest economy in Eastern Europe, was backed up by the presence of about 400,000 Soviet troops. It needed those troops to survive, as East Germany existed only because the Soviet Union was determined to prevent what most Germans wanted: a unified Germany.

The most notable development in East Germany after it was established in 1949 was the building of the Berlin Wall in 1961. Between the late 1940s and that year, about three million people had fled from East to West Germany, including many of East Germany's youngest and best educated people. The Berlin Wall (and miles of barbed wire and watchtowers along the West German border) stopped that flow. Escape attempts continued after 1961, but most failed; about two hundred people were killed trying to escape between 1961 and 1989.

To the east, Bulgaria was a loyal Soviet ally struggling under the dictatorship of Todor Zhivkov. Romania managed to establish a degree of independence under Nicolae Ceaucescu, but his brutal regime was harsh and corrupt even by the standards of Eastern Europe. To the south, on the shores of the Adriatic Sea, Albania broke away from Soviet control in 1961, but that did nothing to soften the harsh Stalinist dictatorship of Enver Hoxha. After breaking with the Soviet Union, Hoxha aligned Albania with China until 1978. He broke with China when it began to reform its Maoist system.

ASIA

Aside from China, the major communist regimes in Asia were North Korea, Vietnam, and Cambodia. The communist regime in North Korea was a child of the Cold War. In 1945, the Red Army occupied the Korean peninsula north of the 38th parallel to take the surrender of Japanese troops in the region, a job the United States army was doing south of the 38th parallel. Both armies then were supposed to withdraw from the peninsula; the withdrawal would be followed by elections and creation of a unified and independent Korea. But Cold War tensions got in the way. The Soviet Union and the United States each installed regimes friendly to themselves, a communist state in the north and a non-communist state in the south.

North Korea was headed by a dictator named Kim Il Sung. In 1950, Kim launched an invasion of South Korea in an attempt to unify the country under his rule. A coalition of nations led by the United States but officially under United Nations command repulsed the invasion in a bloody struggle that lasted from 1950 to 1953. The Korean War, which involved communist China on the North Korean side, ended with an uneasy truce rather than a peace treaty. Thereafter, North Korea continued as a rigid Stalinist regime under Kim's dictatorial control.

Vietnam, like Korea, was divided by the Cold War into a communist north and non-communist south. In Vietnam the communist movement was led by an able and ruthless politician named Ho Chi Minh. After 1946 Ho combined his struggle for communism with the Vietnamese struggle for independence from France, the colonial power in Vietnam since the nineteenth century. His forces finally defeated the French after an eight-year war that ended in 1954. The settlement gave the communists control of Vietnam north of the 17th parallel, while the French and their anti-communist Vietnamese allies withdrew to the south. Elections in 1956 were to unify the country, but as in Korea Cold War tensions intervened. Fearing the loss of all of Vietnam to communism, the United States moved to support a non-communist regime in the south. This left Vietnam divided between two hostile regimes.

Taking advantage of discontent in South Vietnam caused by poverty and corruption, North Vietnam encouraged, supported, and quickly took over a rebellion against the American-backed South Vietnamese government. By the early 1960s the rebellion in the south was a serious threat to the government, and in 1965 United States combat troops entered the war. American troops remained in the field against communist forces until 1973, but were unable to defeat the North Vietnamese troops and the local rebels. After U.S. forces withdrew from Vietnam, a final North Vietnamese push overwhelmed the South Vietnamese regime in 1975. Vietnam became a unified and communist country, although Ho Chi Minh, who died in 1969, did not live to see his final victory.

The communist victory did not bring the promised prosperity to Vietnam. The Vietnamese government proved to be inefficient and often corrupt. Its prison and "reeducation" camps for former South Vietnamese officials and anybody who spoke against communist rule gave Vietnam one of the world's worst human rights records. Collectivization of agriculture in the south backfired so badly that the policy was reversed, but only after food production plummeted and Vietnam had to import rice to feed itself. The Vietnamese government added to the burden on its people when it sent its soldiers into neighboring Cambodia. The Vietnamese troops remained for over a decade, at great cost to Vietnam and its people. This policy in turn led to a short but costly war with China in 1979. By the 1980s many people were fleeing Vietnam in search of a better life.

What happened in Vietnam paled beside events in Cambodia, where communist forces overran the country in 1975. The communist forces in Cambodia were called the Khmer Rouge, and they turned out to be among the most brutal and fanatical people who have ever ruled any country. The Khmer Rouge were determined to build a new communist society from scratch. Their first step was to drive several million people from the cities into the countryside. This was accompanied by a policy of killing anybody suspected of cooperating with the old regime, as well as hundreds of thousands of people who were deemed uncooperative or potentially so. Uncounted others died from lack of food, inadequate housing, and cruel and callous treatment. The name of the Khmer Rouge leader, Pol Pot, became synonomous with terror and genocide. Between 1 and 2 million Cambodians died in the Khmer Rouge "killing fields," perhaps as much as one fourth of the population. It was an unparalleled reign of terror.

The killing continued until the 1978 Vietnamese invasion, which drove the Khmer Rouge back into the jungle and brought a rival group of Cambodian communists to power. That government, whatever its faults, was incomparably better than what had preceeded it. However, the new Cambodian government was unable to defeat the Khmer Rouge, which continued a sporadic guerrilla war.

LATIN AMERICA

Marxism had a long history in Latin America, where poverty and inequality seemed to offer ample opportunity for revolutionaries. By the mid-1920s, communist parties existed in several countries, including Mexico, Cuba, Argentina, and Brazil. For decades they were unable to make much headway in a region often dominated by conservative military regimes. However, Marxist groups finally managed to seize power in three small countries: Cuba, Nicaragua, and Grenada.

By far the most important communist regime in Latin America was in Cuba. Communism came to Cuba after a revolutionary movement led by Fidel Castro overthrew the dictatorship of Fulgencio Batista in 1959. At the time, Castro was not a communist, although several of his movement's leaders were, including his brother Raul. But over the next two years Castro moved toward communism, driven largely by his desire to completely overhaul Cuban society and his hostility toward the United States. Castro's right-hand man, a charismatic revolutionary named Che Guevara, spoke for many Cuban Marxists when he denounced the United States as "the great enemy of mankind."

As Cuba drew closer to the Soviet Union, the United States in 1961 sponsored an invasion of the island by anti-Castro exiles. The invasion was a complete failure and drove Cuba even closer to the Soviet Union. The next year, the most dangerous crisis of the Cold War developed when the Soviet Union attempted to place nuclear missiles in Cuba. Such missiles had the range to hit targets in the southern and eastern United States. President John F. Kennedy ordered the U.S. Navy to blockade Cuba and demanded that all the Soviet missiles be removed. For thirteen days in October 1962, the Cuban Missile Crisis brought the world to the brink

Cuban leader Fidel Castro addresses his supporters in 1959, soon after he came to power.

of nuclear war. Finally, the Soviet Union backed down.

Cuba became one of the Soviet Union's most effective supporters. Castro did what he could to spread communism by supporting revolutionary movements in Latin America and elsewhere in the world. He sent Cuban soldiers to Africa to help communist forces win a civil war in Angola and to Ethiopia to prop up the communist regime there. In return, Cuba received billions of dollars in Soviet economic aid.

Soviet aid was essential to Castro's program of building a communist society in Cuba. The new regime attacked the extremes of wealth and poverty in Cuba by seizing land from wealthy landowners and redistributing it to the peasants. It also seized millions of dollars worth of property owned by foreigners, including Americans. At the same time, Castro introduced many overdue reforms, including improved health care and education.

But neither Castro's programs nor his promises enabled him to deliver on his pledge to make Cuba a prosperous society. The same inefficiences that plagued other centrally controlled economies plagued Cuba's. The same abuses of power that corrupted society in other one-party communist dictatorships corrupted Cuba's. A swollen party bureaucracy snooped and spied on the people while it wasted resources on mismanaged projects and lived far better than ordinary Cubans. Cuba had one of the world's most repressive governments. Free speech, freedom of the press, and independent political parties did not exist. Dissidents were put in prisons where they received brutal treatment.

The second major Marxist regime in Latin

America was in Nicaragua. In 1979, a coalition called the Sandinista front overthrew the repressive dictatorship of Anastasio Somoza. Although the Sandinista movement originally included people of various political viewpoints, after 1979 people who called themselves Marxist-Leninist squeezed out the others. They officially adopted Marxism-Leninism, made Nicaragua a one-party state, and drew closer to both Cuba and the Soviet Union.

However, the Sandinistas did not succeed in turning Nicaragua into a totalitarian society like those in the Soviet Union or Cuba, its main allies. This was largely because opposition forces in Nicaragua received help from the United States. The most significant step the United States took was to fund and support a guerrilla war by a coalition of non-communist forces. This policy was very controversial in the United States, for several reasons. The fighting caused extensive loss of life and property, and led to murder and other atrocities by both sides in Nicaragua. Also, some of the armed groups supported by the United States were former supporters of the Somoza dictatorship. In addition, critics said the United States had no business interfering in the internal affairs of another country. Supporters of U.S. policy stressed that the Sandinistas were attempting to establish a new dictatorship in that troubled country. They also argued that the Sandinistas were trying to undermine neighboring regimes in Central America and that Soviet influence in Nicaragua was a potential threat to the United States.

The same year that the Sandinistas came to power in Nicaragua, a Marxist-Leninist group called the New Jewel Movement seized power on the tiny Caribbean island of Grenada. It immediately aligned itself with Castro's Cuba and the Soviet Union. The same U.S. political analysts who warned about Soviet influence in Nicaragua expressed concern about Grenada. As a result, after a bloody coup led to an even more radical government in 1983, the United States invaded Grenada, overthrew the communists, and replaced them with a non-communist regime.

OTHER MOVEMENTS

During the 1970s, six countries in Africa were ruled by groups calling themselves Marxist-Leninist. The most consistently Marxist of them came to power in Ethiopia in 1974 in a violent coup that overthrew the emperor of that country, Haile Selassie. By the late 1970s the Ethiopian regime was solidly in the Soviet camp and was supported by thousands of Cuban troops. However, economic problems and ethnic divisions tore Ethiopia apart.

Other regimes that called themselves Marxist came to power in Angola, Mozambique, and Madagascar in Africa, and Laos and Afghanistan in Asia. Elsewhere, other Marxist groups struggled to gain power. The most vigorous of these was the Shining Path group in Peru. However, its reputation for fanaticism, violence, and murder left the Shining Path with far more critics, even among Marxists, than it had supporters or friends.

In the end, the future of Marxism did not depend on these minor experiments but on developments in the two great communist powers: the Soviet Union and the People's Republic of China. And what happened in those countries shook the movement founded by Karl Marx to its very roots.

CHAPTER NINE

CRISIS AND COLLAPSE

By the late 1970s, most of the world's Marxist regimes were having serious difficulties. The basic problem was that the combination of central economic planning and political dictatorship that governed Marxist countries was unable to compete with the free enterprise and political democracy that predominated in the West. Central planning stifled individual initiative and was painfully slow in making use of new technologies. As a result, the socialist economies lagged behind many of their non-socialist neighbors. Instead of abundance, Marxist planned economies were delivering endless shortages.

Marxist societies also suffered from rampant corruption. Because of shortages of almost everything, consumers, factory managers, and officials had to resort to bribery and other illegal activities to get what they needed. Those with power, unrestrained by a free press and democratic institutions that could force them from office, used that power for personal benefit. Soviet party leaders lived in luxury apartments, shopped in special stores, received medical treatment in special hospitals, and enjoyed vacation homes and resorts reserved especially for them. As one bitterly ironic Soviet joke put it, "We have communism, but not for everybody." And what was true in the Soviet Union applied, to a greater or lesser degree, to other communist societies. It was all a far cry from the equality promised in *The Communist Manifesto*.

Repression was another common denominator of all Marxist societies. One-party dictatorships could be maintained only if those who dissented were silenced and access to information was controlled. However, by the 1970s the repression was far less severe than in the past in the Soviet Union. In Eastern Europe, some regimes were markedly less oppressive than others. Even in China, the end of the Cultural Revolution and Mao's passing brought about a less hysterical atmosphere. Yet in all communist states, individual lives continued to be regulated and controlled, and basic freedoms were denied.

While some communist regimes, such as those in Poland and Czechoslovakia, would almost certainly have collapsed immediately without Soviet military backing, in the Soviet Union itself the regime still had a significant base of support. Whatever its flaws, it had led the country through World War II and raised the nation's standard of living considerably since the Stalin era. Millions of people, particularly those connected to the Communist Party apparatus, had a stake in the system. And three generations of propaganda had convinced millions more that the Soviet system was better than the capitalist systems of the West. In China, a country with an authoritarian tradition more than two thousand years older than Mao's Marxism, the Communist Party also still had some popular support.

However, both countries were about to change directions. Leaders in both societies realized that many of their old policies had failed, and they sought new solutions to their problems.

CHINA

When Deng Xiaoping came to power in China in 1978, he began a process of reform designed to reverse most of the policies of the Cultural Revolution and modernize China along rational and systematic lines. Those policies quickly led China far away from Maoism and, many would argue, from Marxism.

Deng's program was called the Four Modernizations—of agriculture, industry, science and technology, and national defense. The key to Deng's approach was his belief that CCP policies should be practical and effective. He was not concerned that they necessarily conform to communist ideology and theory. As Deng put it, he did not care about the color of a cat, so long as it could catch mice.

Deng was limited in what he could do as long as Mao's reputation stood unchallenged. In the Soviet Union during the 1950s, Nikita Khrushchev had to deflate Stalin before he could undertake major reforms; now, in China during the 1970s, Deng Xiaoping had to deflate Mao and Maoism. The process of de-Maoization began shortly after Mao's death and

As leaders of the world's greatest Communist powers in the 1980s, Mikhail Gorbachev of the Soviet Union and Deng Xiaoping of China tried to find solutions to growing problems.

[150]

continued gradually until 1981, when the CCP issued a report called "Resolution on the History of Mao's Contributions and Mistakes." It praised Mao for his contributions until the mid-1950s. It then denounced both the Great Leap Forward and the Cultural Revolution, often in bitter language. Soon, the new name for the Cultural Revolution was "Ten Years of Great Castastrophe."

As Deng was devaluing Mao's reputation, he was reversing the dead leader's policies. Nowhere were the changes more radical than in agriculture. Over a period of about five years, the collective farm system was abolished. Although peasants were not permitted to own their land, they were given long-term leases that amounted to almost the same thing. After delivering a quota of their crop to the state to pay for their leases, peasants could sell the rest of that crop on the open market. This incentive to make money, which Mao would have denounced as "capitalist," was a stunning success. Food production soared, enabling China to feed itself. By 1984, socialist agriculture had disappeared from China.

Deng also permitted people to begin small businesses, and they did so by the hundreds of thousands. The new slogan of the 1980s was "To Get Rich Is Glorious," which would have been heresy in Mao's day. Beginning in the mid-1980s, foreign companies were invited to build factories in China, in several "special economic zones." There they hired local Chinese at low wages and often provided very poor working conditions. This return of foreign capitalists to China would have horrified Mao, but to Deng it was a practical way to bring needed investment and technology to China.

However, Deng found that reform could lead to trouble. The problem was that some Chinese, particularly intellectuals and students, believed in political as well as economic reform. They wanted what they called the "Fifth Modernization": democracy. Pressure for political reform began as early as 1979, but Deng used harsh measures to crush the pro-democracy groups.

In the spring of 1989, matters got out of hand. A series of student demonstrations in Beijing in April ballooned into a movement that saw as many as one million students occupying Tiananmen Square, the central plaza in the city. The students were supported by all kinds of people in Beijing, and soon there were millions of demonstrators. The demonstrations continued through May into June. The government then struck with ferocious and overwhelming force. Thousands of soldiers, backed by tanks and other armored vehicles, attacked the demonstrators. Nobody knows how many were killed, but the toll probably ran into the thousands. After the demonstrators were crushed, a reign of terror swept China as Deng and the CCP leadership tried to crush all vestiges of pro-democracy activity.

The repression left the Chinese Communist Party in firm control of China. However, it was highly debatable whether China still had a communist society. The overwhelming majority of the population was made up of peasants who operated as tiny capitalists, buying and selling in the free market. Millions of non-farmers were involved in small businesses. Foreign capitalist firms operated in the special economic zones. Some Chinese were getting richer while others remained poor. The only part of the economy still controlled by the state was heavy industry. But by the 1990s the state factories suffered from poor management and technical backwardness and continually operated at a loss. China's successful factories were run and owned by small private Chinese businesses or by foreign corporations.

In other words, by the 1990s Chinese communism consisted of the dictatorship of the Communist Party and little else. Deng's reforms, while bringing prosperity to China, did so by scrapping most communist policies. A communist political dictatorship backed by military steel still encased the country from the outside; but inside, the communist economic core was gone.

THE SOVIET UNION

By the time Leonid Brezhnev died in 1982, millions of Soviet citizens no longer believed in their government. They saw it as corrupt and unable to solve the nation's growing problems.

Brezhnev was succeeded by Yuri Andropov, an aging and ailing party leader who died after fifteen months in office. While Andropov at least tried to begin making reforms, his successor, a long-time Brezhnev associate named Konstantin Chernenko, did little but try to hold the line. When Chernenko died in 1985 after barely a year in office, the Soviet leadership finally turned to a younger man to try to get their country out of its decades-long slump. His name was Mikhail Gorbachev, and his rise to power began a new and tumultuous era in the history of the Soviet Union and Marxism.

Gorbachev was a convinced Marxist-Leninist who believed the Soviet Union's system needed reform, but still could be fixed. He did not come into office with a comprehensive plan to overhaul Soviet society. After he took office and realized how serious his country's problems were, however, Gorbachev gradually developed more far-reaching policies. Four Russian terms summed up his program: *perestroika* (restructuring), *glasnost* (openness), *demokratizatsia* (democratization), and *novoye myshlenie* (new thinking).

These terms were not precise, and it is important to understand what they meant and what they did *not* mean. *Perestroika* mostly concerned the economy. It assumed that the Soviet Union's socialist planned economy had to be modernized and made more efficient. It did not mean dismantling the Soviet economy and replacing it with capitalism. *Glasnost* meant a major reduction in censorship in the Soviet Union, including more freedom of expression and greater honesty in reporting the country's difficulties. It did not mean full freedom of expression or the abolition of censorship. *Demokratizatsia* meant allowing limited choice within the communist system, such as more than one candidate for party posts. It most certainly did not mean multiparty democracy as practiced in the West. *Novoye myshlenie* (new thinking) referred to foreign policy and meant an end to the arms race and the Cold War. It assumed that capitalist and communist states could coexist and cooperate rather than compete and threaten each other. It did not mean, at least before 1989, that communism in Eastern Europe should be allowed to collapse.

Gorbachev moved slowly during his first year and a half in office, in part because he believed that relatively minor changes could fix the Soviet Union's problems. In addition, he faced powerful resistance to reform from within the Communist Party. Not until 1986, after a disastrous explosion at the Chernobyl nuclear power plant in the Ukraine spread radioactive poisons over thousands of square miles of Soviet territory, did Gorbachev increase the pace of reform. He seemed to have realized then that he needed more drastic measures to solve the problems the Soviet Union faced.

In 1987 Gorbachev announced a series of major economic reforms. One allowed people to set up private businesses for the first time since the 1920s. Another decreased the power of the central planners over Soviet factories. The next year the Soviet Union began converting some military factories to civilian production. In 1989, Gorbachev announced a plan to allow farmers to lease land for private use. This would effectively abolish collective farms and, as Gorbachev optimistically put it, make the farmers once again the "masters of the land."

Glasnost also expanded quickly after 1987. Soon the Soviet people had access to books, films, and radio broadcasts that gave them information and entertainment long denied them. Some of the new information was about the Soviet Union's history since 1917, and it exposed the lies the government had been telling the people for three generations. Political reforms were equally far-reaching and dramatic, and quickly went beyond what Gorbachev seemed to have intended. In 1989, the Soviet people went to the polls for the country's first reasonably free election since 1917 to elect a new governing body called the Congress of People's Deputies. The election shocked the Communist Party, as many reformers and non-communists overwhelmed their communist opponents. Among those elected was Boris Yeltsin, a former party official who had lost his job in 1987 when he criticized Gorbachev for moving too slowly with his reforms. The Congress of People's Deputies in turn elected a smaller Supreme Soviet to serve as the country's new parliament. Several well-known reformers won election to that body, including Yeltsin and Andrei Sakharov, the famous dissident.

Gorbachev's greatest successes came from his policy of new thinking. In 1987, Gorbachev and U.S. president Ronald Reagan signed a historic arms-control treaty that eliminated intermediate-range nuclear missiles from Europe. In 1988, in a speech to the United Nations General Assembly, Gorbachev made it clear that the Soviet Union wanted to co-operate with the West in solving problems like damage to the world environment. He also stressed that no amount of arms could give his or any other nation security. And in February 1989 he took another step to improve relations with both the West and some of his country's next-door neighbors. He kept his pledge to remove all Soviet troops from Afghanistan, a country the Soviet Union had invaded in 1979 to keep the unpopular Afghan communist government in power.

However, Gorbachev soon ran into difficulties. *Perestroika* did not produce a more productive economy. The reforms were introduced piecemeal. Sometimes they did not go far enough; at other times they were undermined by contradictory decrees. At every step Gorbachev and his team faced opposition from powerful, conservative party leaders and from thousands of officials who resisted change.

As a result of these and other problems, Gorbachev's reforms caused the old centrally controlled economic system to collapse faster than a new market economy could take root. Shortages of goods became worse, and prices skyrocketed in the small but growing free-market sector. Factories fired unnecessary employees in an attempt to become more efficient, and for the first time since the 1920s Soviet workers faced unemployment. By 1989 the system that brought food from the farms to the cities was falling apart, and serious food shortages developed. Food rationing began in many cities. People roamed the streets and traveled from city to city looking for food. Angry workers went on strike.

Glasnost and *demokratizatsia* added fuel to the fire. Now that people could obtain information and speak out about their grievances, the bitterness that for years had been kept under wraps by Soviet totalitarianism burst into the open. Despite the official ban that lasted until 1990, people began to organize non-communist political parties. In 1990, voters in local elections across the country voted the communists out of power. Non-communist reformers swept to victory in both Moscow and Leningrad, the country's most important cities.

The most dangerous aspect of this outburst of free expression was the nationalities problem. The Soviet Union in reality was little more than the old pre-1917 Russian empire. Almost half of its population was non-Russian, people whose ancestors had been conquered by Russia over a period of five hundred years. Many of them wanted to break away from Soviet control, which to them was nothing more than Russian control. Making matters more complicated, many of the over one-hundred nationalities in the Soviet Union hated each other more than they disliked the Russians. Gorbachev found himself obliged to control nationalities that wanted to break away from the Soviet Union, while at the same time he had to manage conflicts between various minority groups that sometimes led to bloody fighting.

The mounting problems caused Gorbachev's personal popularity to plunge. Conservatives in the Communist Party criticized him for allowing the country to disintegrate. Radical reformers—led by Boris Yeltsin, who quit the Communist Party in 1990—criticized him for going too slowly with reform. In fact, Gorbachev was far more popular in the West, where he was viewed as a brave reformer and a man of peace, than he was in the Soviet Union. A popular joke summed up the problem:

Question: "What is the difference between the Soviet Union and the United States?

Answer: In the United States, Gorbachev probably would be elected President.

Gorbachev's attempt to save Soviet communism was made even more difficult by events in Eastern Europe. In April 1989, the stalemate between Solidarity and the communist government in Poland began to break. The government agreed to re-legalize the union and permit free elections. The communists calculated that their nationwide organization would enable them to defeat Solidarity, which had no political organization or experience. The results of the election for a new parliament stunned the world: Solidarity completely routed the communists. By

August the country had a non-communist prime minister and most of the cabinet also was non-communist. During the next year, the last vestiges of communism were swept away.

Meanwhile, communism gradually crumbled in Hungary. Reforms began in January 1989, and by October the Communist Party had dissolved. The unrest quickly spread to the remaining Soviet satellites. On November 9, 1989, the communist government in East Germany opened the Berlin Wall in a last-ditch attempt to save itself. It was not successful, and by the end of the year the only question was whether East Germany would continue independent or reunite with West Germany to form one country. On November 10 the communist government of dictator Todor Zhivkov fell in Bulgaria. Czechoslovakia set up its first non-communist-dominated government since 1948 on December 10.

All of this was accomplished without serious violence. In Romania, however, the communist dictator Nicholae Ceaucescu attempted to crush the anti-communist forces with his dreaded secret police. A short, fierce civil war followed, during which Ceaucescu and his wife, his closest political ally, were captured, tried, and executed. The collapse of the Soviet bloc left only two communist regimes in Eastern Europe: Yugoslavia and Albania. In Yugoslavia, communism came to an end when the country dissolved into civil war in 1991, while in Albania the communist regime gradually fell apart that year.

In the Soviet Union, the Gorbachev government did nothing to stop the communist collapse of 1989. Gorbachev did not want those governments to fall; but when they began to collapse, he realized that the price of stopping the process would be too high. Military intervention would have cost billions of dollars and tens of thousands of lives. It would have crippled reform at home and destroyed Gorbachev's foreign policy of new thinking. He therefore accepted the loss of Eastern Europe and concentrated instead on saving communism in the Soviet Union.

It proved to be an impossible task. The process of change Gorbachev's policies had unleashed already had run far beyond what he had intended. Yet radical reformers were accusing him of holding back necessary change. On the other side of the political fence, conservatives in the Communist Party were convinced that the reforms were destroying both communism as a system and the Soviet Union as a country. They made a last-ditch stand to preserve the old system on August 18, 1991, when a group of conservatives seized control of the government and placed Gorbachev under house arrest at his vacation home on the Black Sea coast.

The coup attempt failed. Although most Soviet citizens passively watched events unfold, hundreds of thousands took action. Protesters filled the streets, especially in Moscow and Leningrad. The leader of the resistance was Gorbachev's rival, Boris Yeltsin, who just two months earlier had become the first freely elected president of the Russian republic.

Partly because of poor planning and partly because of the popular resistance, the Soviet army hesitated in carrying out its orders to disperse the crowds with force. That delay was fatal to the coup, which then began to fall apart. Within three days it was all over. Gorbachev was back in Moscow as president of the Soviet Union.

Russian leader Boris Yeltsin flashes a victory sign
to supporters after the failed coup of 1991.
Within months, the Soviet Communist Party
and the Soviet Union itself would collapse.

He did not retain his post for long. The coup was the hammer blow that shattered both the old communist order and the Soviet Union. First the remnants of communist power were swept away. Party officials were thrown out of their offices, and their files were seized. Statues of communist heroes were torn from their pedestals and dumped in the streets. Cities and towns were renamed, among them Leningrad, which reverted to its pre-revolutionary name of St. Petersburg. Gorbachev, who seemed to be in a daze as events unfolded ever more rapidly around him, bowed to reality and resigned his post as party leader.

With communism dead, the Soviet Union itself collapsed soon afterward. Since the late 1980s the republics of Latvia, Lithuania, and Estonia had been attempting to secede from the union. Barely two weeks after the coup, the weakened Soviet government officially recognized their independence. Gorbachev then began a desperate attempt to keep the rest of the old union together. But the forces tearing the Soviet Union apart were far too many and far too strong. Early in December, Boris Yeltsin and leaders from Ukraine and Belorussia (Belarus) announced the formation of what they called the Commonwealth of Independent States—a loosely organized union of independent states. Less than two weeks later, the Commonwealth was formally constituted by eleven of the former Soviet republics, with only Latvia, Lithuania, Estonia, and Georgia remaining outside. On December 25, Mikhail Gorbachev, with nothing more to govern, resigned as president of the now nonexistent Soviet Union.

The red flag with its hammer and sickle, the symbol of Soviet communism, was lowered from over the Kremlin at 7:32 P.M., to be replaced by the white, blue, and red flag of the Russian republic. The first and mightiest society based on the ideas of Karl Marx had passed into history.

FULL CIRCLE

Marxism produced a century and a half of failed predictions and unkept promises. It began as the doctrine of a small group of idealistic intellectuals who were unable to translate their ideas into political power. When, after Marx and Engels died, Marxists finally did come to power, they did not do it in the way Marxism's founders had predicted. Vladimir Lenin led his Marxist Bolshevik Party to power in Russia, a country that most Marxists agreed was not ready for socialism as Marx had described it. Then, instead of spreading westward to the advanced industrialized countries of Europe as Marxist theory suggested, the Marxist revolution spread eastward to China, an unindustrialized country in Asia. Marxism's only conquests in Europe outside the Soviet Union came in the wake of the Red Army's westward advance at the end of World War II. But these Marxist societies were established by force, not through workers' revolutions as Marx had predicted.

In addition, as Marxism spread eastward into countries lacking democratic traditions, it became increasingly dictatorial and, eventually, totalitarian. Some Marxists in the West rejected the totalitarian forms of Marxism that evolved in Russia and China, but Soviet and Chinese Marxism dominated world Marxism because they controlled large countries with millions of people.

Eventually Marxism would govern more than twenty countries, in both hemispheres and on four continents. At its peak, one third of the world's population lived under Marxist rule. But nowhere could Marxists create the type of society Marx advocated. Instead of enjoying wealth and prosperity, the people of Marxist countries endured poverty and tyranny. Rather than overwhelming capitalism with proof that there was a better way to live, Marxist societies performed so badly that capitalism, with all its faults, looked better than ever. Instead of establishing ideal societies where justice and fairness ruled, Marxism created some of the most monstrous and murderous regimes that ever existed.

By 1991 most of the world's ruling Marxist parties had been swept from power. The most dramatic defeats outside Eastern Europe and the Soviet Union occurred in Nicaragua and Ethiopia. In Nicaragua, misguided economic policies, mismanagement and corruption, and the expense of trying to put down the U.S.-sponsored anti-government guerrillas drained the Nicaraguan economy. When the Sandinistas gambled on free elections in 1990, they were decisively defeated by a non-communist coalition. Torn by civil war, Ethiopia's Marxist government collapsed during 1991.

Where they still ruled, Marxist regimes were abandoning many of their principles, or barely hanging on. In China, the party had to reject most of its socialist policies and rely on capitalist methods to make economic progress. In Cuba, where Fidel Castro refused to make concessions to democracy or capitalism, the country's economy continued to crumble while Cubans both inside and outside the country waited for Castro's death so that reform could finally begin. In Vietnam, as the country sank deeper into poverty, the government looked to the capitalist nations of the world for help. In North Korea, Cambodia, Laos, and Afghanistan, Asia's other remaining Marxist states, the future for communism looked no better.

Wherever Marxism had governed, it had failed. For years Karl Marx had contemptuously dismissed rival philosophies as unrealistic and utopian, but rarely had a philosophy proved so impossible to translate into reality as the one that bore his name. By the 1990s, Marxism had come full circle. It flourished only where it had begun: among intellectuals in the industrialized West. They tinkered with new versions of Marxism and tried to explain why the older versions had failed to produce better societies. But they convinced few people in the general population and remained as far from power as Marx and Engels in their most discouraging days. Marx once wrote that history repeats itself, "the first time as tragedy, the second as farce." That observation proved to be an appropriate epitaph to the history of a movement whose time had come and gone.

NOTES

Chapter Two

1. Sylvain Marechal, *Manifesto of Equals*, in *Modern Socialism*, Massimo Salvadori, editor (New York: Harper and Row, 1968), p. 57.
2. Cited in George Lichteim, *The Origins of Socialism* (New York: Frederick A. Praeger, 1969), pp. 46–47.

Chapter Three

1. Karl Marx, *Theses on Feuerbach*, in *Marx and Engels: Basic Writings on Politics and Philosophy*, Lewis S. Feurer, editor (Garden City and New York: Doubleday & Company, 1959), p. 245.
2. Karl Marx and Friedrich Engels, *The Communist Manifesto* in *The Essential Works of Marxism*, Arthur Mendel, editor (New York: Bantam Books, 1961), p. 113.
3. Friedrich Engels, "Origin of the Family, Private Prop-

erty and the State," in *Selected Works*, vol. 3 (Progress Publishers), p. 266.
4. Friedrich Engels, "Karl Marx's Funeral," in *Marx's Concept of Man*, by Erich Fromm (New York: Frederick Unger, 1970), p. 258.

Chapter Four

1. Cited in Rolf H. W. Theen, *Lenin: Genesis and the Development of a Revolutionary* (Princeton: Princeton University Press, 1973), p. 34.
2. Cited in Michael Kort, *The Soviet Colossus: A History of the USSR* (New York: Charles Scribner's Sons, 1985), p. 66.
3. Thomas Riha, editor, *Readings in Russian Civilization*, second edition, revised (Chicago: University of Chicago Press, 1969), p. 515.
4. Isaac Deutscher, *The Prophet Armed: Trotsky 1879–1921* (New York: Vintage, 1965), pp. 513–14.

Chapter Five

1. Robert V. Daniels, editor, *A Documentary History of Communism* (updated revised edition), vol. 1: "Communism in Russia" (Hanover and London: University Press of New England), p. 230.
2. Victor Kravchenko, *I Chose Justice* (New York: Charles Scribner's Sons, 1950), pp. 99–100.
3. Thomas Riha, editor, *Readings in Russian Civilization* (second edition, revised), vol. III: Soviet Russia, 1917–1963 (Chicago and London: University of Chicago Press, 1969), p. 549.

Chapter Six

1. Nikita Khrushchev, "Khrushchev's Secret Speech," in *Khrushchev Remembers*, Strobe Talbot, editor (New York: Bantam Books, 1971), p. 620.

Chapter Seven

1. Cited in the Introduction to *Karl Marx on Colonialism and Modernization*, Shlomo Avineri, editor (New York and Garden City: Anchor Books, 1969), pp. 14–15.
2. Mao Zedong, "Report on an Investigation of the Peasant Movement in Hunan," in *China in Revolution*, Vera Simone, editor (Greenwich, CT: Fawcett, 1968), p. 170.
3. Cited in Jene Grasso, Jay P. Corrin, and Michael Kort, *Modernization and Revolution in China* (Armonk, N.Y., and London: M. E. Sharpe, 1991), p. 161.
4. Stuart Schram, editor, *Chairman Mao Talks to the People, Talks and Letters: 1958–1971* (New York: Pantheon Books, 1974), pp. 92–93.
5. Mark Selden, *The People's Republic of China: A Documentary History of Revolutionary Change* (New York: Monthly Review Press, 1978), p. 413.
6. Cited in Roxane Witke, *Comrade Chiang Ching* (Boston: Little, Brown, & Co., 1972), p. 325.
7. Liang Heng and Judith Shapiro, *Son of the Revolution* (New York: Vintage Books, 1984), pp. 132–33.

Chapter Eight

1. *The New York Times*, January 4, 1992.

SUGGESTED READING

On Marx

Isaiah Berlin, *Karl Marx: His Life and Environment*. London, Oxford, and New York: Oxford University Press, 1963.

M. M. Bober, *Karl Marx's Interpretation of History*. New York: Norton, 1965.

On Marxism in general

Erich Fromm, *Marx's Concept of Man*. New York: Frederick Unger, 1966.

David McLellan, *Marxism After Marx*. New York: Harper and Row, 1979.

C. Wright Mills, *The Marxists*. New York: Dell, 1962.

On Lenin, Stalin, and the Soviet Union

Geoffrey Hosking, *The First Socialist Society*. Cambridge, Mass.: Harvard University Press, 1985.

Michael Kort, *The Soviet Colossus*. New York: Scribner's, 1985.

Rolf H. W. Theen. *Lenin*. Princeton, N.J.: Princeton University Press, 1973.

Adam Ulam, *Stalin*. New York: Viking, 1973.

On Mao Zedong and the People's Republic of China

John King Fairbank, *The United States and China* (Fourth Edition, Enlarged). Cambridge, Mass.: Harvard University Press, 1983.

June Grasso, Jay P. Corrin, and Michael Kort, *Revolution and Modernization in China*, Armonk, N.Y.: M. E. Sharpe, 1991.

Edward E. Rice, *Mao's Way*. Berkeley: University of California Press, 1974.

Edgar Snow, *Red Star Over China*. New York: Bantam, 1978.

On the decline of Marxism

Zbigniew Brzezinski, *The Grand Failure: The Birth and Death Of Communism in the Twentieth Century*. New York: Macmillan, 1990.

Nick Eberstadt, *The Poverty of Communism*. New Brunswick, N.J.: Transaction Publishers, 1988.

CHRONOLOGY

1818	Karl Marx born
1848	Marx and Engels publish *The Communist Manifesto*
1864	First International founded
1867	First volume of *Capital* published
1870	Valdimir Ulyanov (Lenin) born
1879	Joseph Stalin and Leon Trotsky born
1883	Karl Marx dies
1883	First Russian Marxist group (Liberation of Labor) formed
1889	Second International founded
1893	Mao Zedong born
1902	Lenin publishes *What Is to Be Done?*
1903	Russian Social Democrats (Marxists) split into Bolshevik and Menshevik factions
1917	Bolsheviks led by Lenin seize power in Russia
1918	Bolshevik Party name changed to Communist Party

1919	Third International (Comintern) founded
1922	Stalin chosen Communist Party general secretary
1924	Lenin dies
1924–29	Stalin wins the struggle to succeed Lenin
1929–38	Industrialization, collectivization, and the Great Purge in the Soviet Union
1940	Trotsky murdered
1945–48	Soviet-controlled communists take over countries of Eastern Europe
1948	Yugoslavia, under Tito, breaks from the Soviet bloc
1949	Communist Party led by Mao Zedong wins civil war and takes power in China
1953	Stalin dies
1953–64	Khrushchev reform era in Soviet Union
1956	Khrushchev's destalinization speech; Hungarian revolt crushed
1958–60	Great Leap Forward in China
1959	Fidel Castro seizes power in Cuba
1961	Berlin Wall erected
1962	Cuban Missile Crisis
1964–82	Brezhnev era in the Soviet Union
1966-69	Cultural Revolution in China
1968	Reform movement crushed in Czechoslovakia
1976	Mao dies
1980	Solidarity trade union organized in Poland
1985	Mikhail Gorbachev comes to power in the Soviet Union
1989	Communism collapses in Eastern Europe; pro-democracy movement crushed in China
1991	Soviet Union collapses

INDEX

Page numbers in *italics* refer to illustrations.

Afghanistan, 146, 156, 165
Agriculture, 14, 79-82, *83*, 84, 90, 98, 100, 101, 118-119, 151
Albania, 92, 138, 159
Alexander II, Tsar, 44
Alienation, 36-37
Andropov, Yuri, 153
Angola, 9, 144, 146
Antithesis, 30
Argentina, 142

Babeuf, François Noël, 15-16
Bakunin, Michael, 40
Batista, Fulgencio, 142
Belorussia (Belarus), 162
Beria, Lavrenti, 94, 99
Berlin Wall, 138, 159
Bernstein, Eduard, 47
Blanqui, Louis-Auguste, 28
Bolsheviks, 7, 8, 54-55, 58, 59, 62-73, 90, 109, 110, 163

Bourgeoisie, 36, 38, 75
Brazil, 142
Brest-Litovsky, Treaty of (1918), 64
Brezhnev, Leonid, 103–105, 153
Brezhnev Doctrine, 105
Bukharin, Nikolai, 77, 86
Bulgaria, 92, 159

Cambodia, 132, 138, 140, 141, 165
Capital (Marx), 28-29, 49, 52
Capitalism, 7-8, 12, 28, 34, 36-37, 55-56, 164
Castro, Fidel, 142, *143*, 164-165
Ceausescu, Nicolae, 138, 159
Chen Duxiu, 110
Chen Yun, 123
Chernenko, Konstantin, 153
Chernov, Victor, 65
Chernyshevsky, Nicholas, 52, 54

Chiang Kaishek, 109, 111, 114, 115
Chinese Communist Party (CCP), 110, 111, 113-119, 124, 131, 149, 151, 152
Class consciousness, 38
Class struggle, 33-34
Cold War, 93, 104, 139, 154
Collectivization of agriculture, 79-82, 83, 84, 90, 98, 118-119
Colonialism, 107-108
Commonwealth of Independent States, 162
Communism, 7, 39, 91-92, 99, 132-134, 136-141, 148, 154, 158-160, 165
Communist International, 72-73
Communist Manifesto, The (Marx and Engels), 8, 9, 27, 42, 148
Communist Party of the Soviet Union, 72, 85, 86, 88, 101, 155, 158, 160, 162
Condition of the Working Class in England 1844 (Engels), 26
Corruption, 40, 71, 147-148
Cuba, 9, 132, 142, 143, 144, 164-165
Cuban Missile Crisis, 102, 125, 142-143
Cultural Revolution, 125-126, 127, 128-131, 148, 151
Czechoslovakia, 92, 134, 135, 136, 148, 159

De-Maoization, 149, 151
Democracy, 13-14, 38
Demokratizatsia (democratization), 154, 157
Deng Xiaoping, 131, 149, 150, 151-153
Destalinization, 98-99, 104, 124, 149
Dialectics, 29-31

Dictatorship of the proletariat, 38, 101
Dubcek, Alexander, 134, 136

East Germany (Democratic Republic of Germany), 92, 137-138, 159
Economy, 9, 12, 39, 68-70, 79, 85, 105, 119-123, 147, 151-157
Engels, Friedrich, 8, 16, 24, 25, 26-29, 39-42, 44, 45
Equality, 13
Estonia, 162
Ethiopia, 132, 144, 146, 164
Exploitation, 36, 37

Five-Year Plans, 79, 85
Formosa (Taiwan), 117
Fourier, Charles, 16, 19, 21
Four Modernizations, 149
French Revolution, 15, 16, 18, 24

General Will, 15
Georgia, 162
German Ideology, The (Marx and Engels), 26
German Social Democratic Party (SPD), 42, 44, 46, 47, 53
Glasnost (openness), 154, 155, 157
Gorbachev, Mikhail, 150, 153-160, 162
Great Leap Forward, 120-125, 151
Great Purge, 86-87
Grenada, 145-146
Guevara, Che, 142
Guomindang (GMD), 109, 110, 113-115, 117

Hegel, Georg Wilhem Friedrich, 24, 29-31
Historical materialism, 31-33
Hitler, Adolf, 90

Ho Chi Minh, 139
Hoxha, Enver, 138
Hua Gofeng, 131
Human will, 114, 116
Hungary, 92, 99, 134, 159

Imperialism, 56
Industrialization, 78-79, 84,
    90, 93, 98
Industrial Revolution, 16-18,
    34
International Workingmen's
    Association (First Interna-
    tional), 42
Iroquois Indians, 39-40

Jiang Qing, 126, 129-131

Kamenev, Lev, 77, 86
Kautsky, Karl, 46
Kennedy, John F., 142
Khmer Rouge, 141
Khrushchev, Nikita, 95-96,
    97, 98-104, 124-125, 149
Kim Il Sung, 139
Korean War, 139
Kronstadt rebellion, 67-68
Kulaks, 69, 81

Labor theory of value, 36
Laos, 146, 165
Latin America, 141-142, 144-
    146
Latvia, 162
Lenin, Vladimir, 51-56, 57,
    58, 59, 62-66, 68, 70-71, 74,
    163
Leninism, 52-56, 71, 72, 89
Li Dazhao, 110, 111
Lin Biao, 126, 130
Lithuania, 162
Liu Shaoqi, 119, 122-123,
    126, 131
Long March, 115, 117

Madagascar, 146
Manchu dynasty, 107, 108

Manifesto of Equals, 15
Mao Zedong, 111, 112, 113-
    117, 119-126, 128-131, 148,
    149, 151
Martov, Julius, 55, 58
Marx, Heinrich, 23
Marx, Jenny, 23, 24, 44
Marx, Karl, 6, 7-8, 12, 13, 16,
    22-24, 26-34, 36-42, 44, 45,
    107-108
Marxism, 8-9, 11, 29-34, 40-
    42, 47, 49-56, 62, 72-73, 88-
    89, 93, 95-96, 98-103, 105,
    106, 109-111, 113-114, 141-
    142, 144-149, 153, 163-165
Marxism-Leninism, 71-73,
    132, 145
Means of production, 32, 36,
    39
Mensheviks, 55, 58, 59, 61-63
Mexico, 142
Mode of production, 31-32,
    41
More, Sir Thomas, 14, 15
Mozambique, 146

Nazi Germany, 90, 91
New Economic Policy (NEP),
    68-70
Nicaragua, 9, 145, 164
Nicholas II, Tsar, 58-60
North Atlantic Treaty Organi-
    zation (NATO), 93
North Korea, 132, 138-139,
    165
Novoye myshlenie (new
    thinking), 154, 156
Nuclear weapons, 100, 102,
    142, 144

Owen, Robert, 16, 20, 21

Paris Commune, 42, 43
Peaceful coexistence, 99-100
Perestroika (restructuring),
    154-156
Permanent revolution, 75

Peru, 146
Plato, 13-15
Plekhanov, Georgi, 49, 58
Poland, 92, 99, 136-137, 148, 158-159
Pol Pot, 141
Populists, 49-50, 53, 54, 59
Prague Spring, 136
Pravda, 10
Private property, 32
Proletariat, 36-38, 40, 53, 56, 59, 75, 113

Quotations of Chairman Mao, 126, 127

Reagan, Ronald, 156
Red Army, 66, 67, 91, 92, 132
Red Guards, 126, 128-130
Religion, 29
Republic, The (Plato), 13
Revisionism, 47
Revolution of 1905, 58-60
Revolutions of 1848, 27-28
Romania, 92, 138, 159
Rousseau, Jean-Jacques, 15, 19

Saint-Simon, Claude Henri, 16-19
Sakharov, Andrei, 104, 105, 156
Sandinista movement, 145, 164
Second Bolshevik Revolution, 77-79
Second International, 47, 73
Second United Front, 115
Secret police, 65, 66, 88, 94-95
Sino-Soviet split, 124-125
Social divisions, 13
Socialism, 7, 8, 12-19, 21, 37-39
Solidarity, 136-137, 158
Somoza, Anastasio, 145
Soviet Jews, 105
Space program, 103
Stalin, Joseph, 66, 71, 74-75, 76, 77-82, 84-91, 93, 95, 98, 104, 124, 133, 149

Substructure of society, 31-33
Sun Yatsen, 109
Superstructure of society, 32-33, 41
Surplus value, 36
Synthesis, 30

Thesis, 30
Tiananmen Square massacre, 152
Tito, Joseph Broz, 133-134
Totalitarianism, 88-91
Trotsky, Leon, 55, 57, 58, 63, 66, 68, 74-75, 77, 87

Ukraine, 83, 162
Ulyanov, Alexander, 51-52
Ulyanov, Vladimir (see Lenin, Vladimir)
United Front strategy, 110-111
United States Constitution, 40-41
Utopia, 14
Utopian socialists, 16-19, 21

Vietnam, 9, 132, 138-141, 165
Virgin lands program, 100, 101

Walesa, Lech, 136
War Communism, 67-69
Warsaw Pact, 93
Westphalen, Ludwig von, 23
Winter Palace, 48
Work day, 14, 17, 21
World Spirit, 30, 31
World War I, 60
World War II, 9, 91, 115, 116

Yanan Way, 116
Yeltsin, Boris, 156, 158, 160, 161, 162
Yugoslavia, 93, 133-134, 159

Zhengfeng, 116
Zhivkov, Todor, 138, 159
Zhou Enlai, 131
Zinoviev, Grigori, 77, 86